At Issue

Corporate Corruption

Other Books in the At Issue Series

At Issue

Corporate Corruption

Sarah Armstrong, Book Editor

GREENHAVEN PRESS
A part of Gale, Cengage Learning

GALE
CENGAGE Learning

Farmington Hills, Mich • San Francisco • New York • Waterville, Maine
Meriden, Conn • Mason, Ohio • Chicago

Judy Galens, *Manager, Frontlist Acquisitions*

© 2016 Greenhaven Press, a part of Gale, Cengage Learning.

Gale and Greenhaven Press are registered trademarks used herein under license.

For more information, contact:
Greenhaven Press
27500 Drake Rd.
Farmington Hills, MI 48331-3535
Or you can visit our Internet site at gale.cengage.com

For product information and technology assistance, contact us at

Gale Customer Support, 1-800-877-4253
For permission to use material from this text or product, submit all requests online at www.cengage.com/permissions.

Further permissions questions can be e-mailed to permissionrequest@cengage.com.

Articles in Greenhaven Press anthologies are often edited for length to meet page requirements. In addition, original titles of these works are changed to clearly present the main thesis and to explicitly indicate the author's opinion. Every effort is made to ensure that Greenhaven Press accurately reflects the original intent of the authors. Every effort has been made to trace the owners of copyrighted material.

LIBRARY OF CONGRESS CATALOGING-IN-PUBLICATION DATA

Corporate corruption (Greenhaven Press)
 Corporate corruption / Sarah Armstrong, book editor.
   pages cm. -- (At issue)
 Includes bibliographical references and index.
 ISBN 978-0-7377-7364-4 (hardcover) -- ISBN 978-0-7377-7365-1 (pbk.)
 1. Corporations--Corrupt practices. 2. Business ethics. 3. Corporate governance.
 I. Armstrong, Sarah, 1979- editor. II. Title.
 HF5387.C66792 2016
 364.16'8--dc23
                                2015026930

Printed in the United States of America
2 3 4 5 6   22 21 20 19 18

Contents

Introduction

On October 29, 2004, Ivor van Heerden, then deputy director of Louisiana State University's Hurricane Center, made the following prediction in an interview with the PBS science program *NOVA*: "A slow-moving Category 3 hurricane or larger will flood the city [of New Orleans, Louisiana]. There will be between 17 and 20 feet of standing water, and New Orleans as we now know it will no longer exist."[1] He went on to discuss the infrastructure problems of the levees and the implications of such a disaster for those living in the city. Ten months later, on August 29, 2005, Hurricane Katrina devastated the city of New Orleans. Perhaps more disconcerting than Heerden's initial prediction, however, was the accuracy with which he foresaw, not just the infrastructure breeches of the city, but the fault lines of a political infrastructure that could have prevented such a disaster from occurring in the first place.

The following year, in the fall of 2006, another storm was brewing, but this was one that would send economic tidal waves across the shores of more than just a single city, deep into the heart of Wall Street, Washington, DC, and as far away as Europe and Asia. And much like the prediction made by Heerden concerning Hurricane Katrina, the economic tsunami that was about to break was portended with chilling accuracy by an economist who has since become known as "Dr. Doom."

On September 7, 2006, Nouriel Roubini stood before a group of government officials, policy makers, and corporate executives at the International Monetary Fund and presented an economic forecast that was as prescient as it was bleak. He said: "My concern today is that the bursting of the housing bubble—we have not seen it yet—is going to lead to broader

---

1. Quoted in "The Man Who Predicted Katrina," *NOVA*, November 22, 2005. www.pbs.org/wgbh/nova/earth/predicting-katrina.html.

systemic banking problems. It is going to start with the subprime lenders—they are already in trouble because of in-
creases in delinquencies and foreclosures—and then it is going
to be transmitted to other banks and financial institutions all
over the country."[2]

Little more than six months later, in March of 2007, HSBC
Holdings—Europe's largest bank—reported significant losses
in its subprime mortgage services division. By the following
month, dozens of American subprime lending institutions began to topple like dominoes.

This was soon followed by the meteoric fall of finance industry giants such as Bear Stearns, Lehman Brothers, Coun-
trywide Financial, and Washington Mutual Bank. Nearly five
million families foreclosed on their homes. More than two
million people would be out of work by the end of 2008. Industrial cities, such as Detroit, found themselves on the brink
of collapse; what began as a housing crisis had now become a
manufacturing crisis, as average Americans saw their wealth
cut in half almost overnight and tightened their spending. It
was the greatest economic disaster Americans had suffered
since the Great Depression (1929–1939).

In the wake of the recession and the government's "bailout" response, known as the Troubled Assets Relief Program
(TARP), a host of theories as to the reason for the economic
collapse began to surface. The predominant narrative focuses
on the intersection of corporate corruption and government
power and theorizes that the crisis could have been prevented
through better federal regulation and oversight. Pulitzer-prize
winning journalist Gretchen Morgenson, coauthor of the book
*Reckless Endangerment: How Outsized Ambition, Greed, and
Corruption Led to Economic Armageddon*, stated that the economic collapse "was the result of actions taken by people at

---

2. Nouriel Roubini, "EconoMonitor Flashback: Roubini's IMF Speech—September 7,
2006," EconoMonitor, September 2, 2010. www.economonitor.com/nouriel/2010/09
/02/economonitor-flashback-roubinis-imf-speech-september-7-2006.

the height of power in both the public and the private sectors, people who continue, even now, to hold sway in the corridors of Washington and Wall Street."[3]

While many pundits blame the so-called Great Recession on the actions of both private industry and government regulators, there are those who see corporate greed and corruption as the primary reason for the economic collapse. These experts point to a number of either illegal, unethical, or negligent activities of private companies—specifically in the financial sector—that fueled and worsened the disaster.

One example is that of Washington Mutual. Infamous for being the largest bank failure in US history, WaMu, as it is known, ultimately met its demise in September 2008. For several years, the bank had been knowingly engaging in rampant fraudulent lending practices, steering low-income customers toward high-interest, high-risk loans they couldn't afford. "The company was setting up thousands, if not millions of borrowers for foreclosure, while booking illusory short-term profits and paying out giant bonuses for its employees and executives,"[4] said Zach Carter in a blog for the Campaign for America's Future. Senator Carl Levin, who chaired a Senate subcommittee responsible for conducting an inquiry into the cause of the 2008 financial crisis, remarked that "Washington Mutual built a conveyor belt that dumped toxic mortgage assets into the financial system like a polluter dumping poison into a river. Using a toxic mix of high-risk lending, lax con-

3. Gretchen Morgenson and Joshua Rosner, *Reckless Endangerment: How Outsized Ambition, Greed, and Corruption Led to Economic Armageddon*. New York: Times Books, 2011, p. xiv.
4. Zach Carter, "WaMu: Rampant Fraud and Financial Collapse," Campaign for America's Future, April 14, 2010. http://ourfuture.org/20100414/wamu-rampant-fraud-and -financial-collapse.

trols and destructive compensation policies, Washington Mutual flooded the market with shoddy loans and securities that went bad."[5]

Commentators who blame corporate greed for the 2008 economic crash often cite Lehman Brothers as another telling example of the corporate maleficence that led to the disaster. The fourth-largest investment bank in the world, Lehman declared bankruptcy the very same month as Washington Mutual, but with even greater disastrous economic consequences. After a quarterly loss of almost $3 billion in early 2008, Lehman was desperate to maintain its market ratings and investor confidence, which were rapidly beginning to wane. Eager to present a favorable financial picture to its stakeholders, the firm had been employing an "accounting sleight of hand known as a Repo 105 transaction . . . drastically reducing its leverage and making its financial picture look better than it really was,"[6] according to Susanne Craig and Mike Spector in a 2010 *Wall Street Journal* article. But the reality was that Lehman no longer had enough financial assets to fund its global operations and, as a result, filed for Chapter 11 bankruptcy protection on September 15, 2008. The Dow Jones Industrial average fell by more than 500 points the same day. Anton Valukas, a former US attorney who conducted the official investigation into Lehman's demise, said, "Everybody got hurt. The entire economy has suffered from the fall of Lehman Brothers . . . the whole world."[7]

While the failure of megabanks such as these point to fraudulent lending practices, devious accounting strategies,

5. Quoted in "Senate Subcommittee Launches Series of Hearings on Wall Street and the Financial Crisis," US Senate Permanent Subcommittee on Investigations, April 12, 2010. www.hsgac.senate.gov/subcommittees/investigations/media/senate-subcommittee-launches-series-of-hearings-on-wall-street-and-the-financial-crisis.

6. Susanne Craig and Mike Spector, "Repos Played a Key Role in Lehman's Demise," *Wall Street Journal*, March 13, 2010. www.wsj.com/articles/SB10001424052748703447104575118150651790066.

7. Quoted in Steve Kroft, "The Case Against Lehman Brothers," *60 Minutes*, April 23, 2012. www.cbsnews.com/news/the-case-against-lehman-brothers-23-04-2012/5.

and simple outright greed as reasons for the global economic downturn, others believe that the main source of the problem originated with the government, either for its misguided monetary policies or its lack of regulation and oversight of the financial industry. This view is perhaps best expressed by financial attorney and author Peter J. Wallison, who argued in a 2011 written dissent to the Financial Crisis Inquiry Commission:

> I believe that the [reason for] the financial crisis was U.S. government housing policy, which led to the creation of 27 million subprime and other risky loans—half of all mortgages in the United States—which were ready to default as soon as the massive 1997–2007 housing bubble began to deflate. If the U.S. government had not chosen this policy path—fostering the growth of a bubble of unprecedented size and an equally unprecedented number of weak and high-risk residential mortgages—the great financial crisis of 2008 would never have occurred.[8]

Much like the city of New Orleans, America's recovery from and prevention against future disaster—geographic or economic—remains a relevant concern. While the United States and Europe have, for the most part, regained financial stability, the Great Recession of 2008 continues to serve as an acute reminder of the presence of greed and corruption inside American corporations and government. The viewpoints in *At Issue: Corporate Corruption* discuss not only the implications of the financial crisis but also other facets of corporate corruption, such as globalism, environmental crime and degradation, and the contentious battle between corporate rights and individual rights being waged in America's courts.

8. Peter J. Wallison and Arthur F. Burns, "Financial Crisis Inquiry Commission Dissenting Statement," FCIC at Stanford Law School, January 2011. http://fcic-static .law.stanford.edu/cdn_media/fcic-reports/fcic_final_report_wallison_dissent.pdf.

Global Efforts to Fight Corruption Are Not Working

Frank Vogl

Frank Vogl is president of Vogl Communications, a Washington, DC-based firm that specializes in financial, media, and governmental consulting. In addition to writing and lecturing widely on the topic of finance and corruption, he is also a cofounder of Transparency International, an international nonprofit, nongovernmental organization working against corruption and bribery.

New research reveals that the majority of the nations that signed the Organisation for Economic Co-operation and Development's Anti-Bribery Convention Act do not actively enforce the agreement and, in many cases, are guilty of violating it. Because such corruption creates an unfair playing field for those who are committed to operating with honesty and integrity, stronger anticorruption initiatives should be implemented in both emerging market countries and those nations that participated in the recent G20 Anti-Corruption Working Group (ACWG). The Group of 20, known as the G20, is the international forum connecting government representatives from twenty major economies— nineteen economically developed countries and the European Union.

It takes two to tango to rob national treasuries and undermine global commerce: the government officials and politicians who take the bribes and, of course, the corporations who pay the bribes.

Just how rotten current conditions are is evident from two new reports—Transparency International's index of bribe taking and a comprehensive OECD [Organisation for Economic Co-operation and Development] analysis of corporate bribe paying.

Transparency International's 2014 Corruption Perceptions Index (CPI) covering 175 countries reveals that more than two-thirds score less than 50 points on a scale, where 100 is fully clean of corruption and 1 is the very opposite.

Monitoring Just How Pervasive Bad Governance Is

If one looks, for example, at emerging market economies, where to an increasing degree governments have publicly pledged to attack corruption, then the picture remains bleak. Levels of perceived corruption in most emerging market countries are very high, with the great majority having CPI scores of less than 50, including the four BRICS [Brazil, Russia, India, and China]. . . .

As a new study by the OECD shows, many companies are willing to shave their profits significantly to pay bribes and win deals.

Many executives at multinational corporations have long acknowledged the significant risks of doing business with government partners in many emerging market countries, but these are so often offset by considerations of both the very large size and especially the potential of these markets.

Wal-Mart, for example, is now engaged in a multi-year, multi-million dollar internal investigation of allegations that its executives paid bribes in a range of emerging market countries, including Mexico, Brazil and India.

Most corporations, I hope, nevertheless find ways to do business honestly, but as a new study by the OECD shows, many companies are willing to shave their profits significantly to pay bribes and win deals.

The OECD reviewed the cases of 400 corporations that have been investigated for bribing foreign government officials—investigations that took place in some of the 41 countries that signed the OECD Anti-Bribery Convention that first came into force in 1998 and that makes it a criminal offense for a company to bribe a foreign government official.

The OECD said that on average the bribes paid equaled 10.9% of the total transaction value and 34.5% of the profits, equal to $13.8 million per bribe.

Only Half the Story

Both the Transparency International and the OECD reports have to be considered with some caution. The CPI is based on a series of well respected opinion polls each year and Transparency International underscores that the results reflect perceptions, not hard facts.

The OECD report covers what is probably just a tiny fraction of the number of companies that have paid bribes or are paying them today.

The problem in part is that the overwhelming majority of the 41 countries that ratified the OECD pact are not enforcing it.

The vast bulk of investigations and prosecutions have been pursued by the U.S. authorities—the Department of Justice and the Securities and Exchange Commission [SEC].

To be sure, the significant rise in U.S. cases has been possible because public prosecutors in an increasing number of countries are quietly sharing evidence with the Americans and cooperating in investigations.

Nevertheless, the two reports underscore the harsh reality that corruption is pervasive and that it is an important distortion in international commerce. Corruption seriously disadvantages those firms that are intent on doing business openly and honestly.

Pressuring the Bad Apples

Pressures need to be placed on the majority of the countries that signed the OECD convention to start enforcing it. This has become a high campaigning priority for Transparency International, which recently announced plans to step-up actions on this front.

Shedding light on such payments [bribes] is important, but it demands the full engagement of the U.S. authorities to be effective.

At the same time, an array of complementary initiatives need to be aggressively pursued to promote more of a transparent and level playing field for international business, free of corruption.

As the CPI shows, some of the countries seen to have the highest levels of perceived corruption are oil exporters: absolutely awful CPI scores of below 20 are seen for such oil exporters as Venezuela, Angola and Guinea-Bissau (all with 19 points), Libya (18), Iraq (16) and Sudan (11).

Legislation has moved forward in Europe to force companies in the extractive industries publicly to disclose their annual royalty payments to foreign governments.

Shedding light on such payments is important, but it demands the full engagement of the U.S. authorities to be effective.

While the 2010 Dodd-Frank Financial Reform Act provided for the SEC to ensure annual reporting on foreign payments by oil, gas and mining companies, the industry has delayed action through the courts and the SEC has shown no enthusiasm to be energetic on this front.

In addition, the Group of 20 [international forum connecting representatives from twenty major economies (nineteen countries and the European Union)] at its mid-November [2014] summit in Australia approved a new "Anti-Corruption Action Plan" with clear commitments to tighten enforcement of regulations to curb both business bribery of officials and money laundering. If action follows rhetoric, then some solid progress could be made in the months to come.

But, perhaps the greatest hope rests in the emerging market countries themselves. Corruption was the major topic in the national elections in India this year and Prime Minister Modi has pledged to act.

In Brazil, an enormous scandal has recently surfaced that may start to clean-up the ways many major construction companies win government contracts and how political parties are illicitly financed.

And then, while the CPI shows a deterioration in perceptions of corruption in China, the aggressive anticorruption campaign being waged by President Xi Jingping may over time start to affect the behavior of both powerful corrupt officials and too many multinational corporations still too willing to bribe their way into deals.

2

Creating a Culture of Integrity Can Mitigate Corporate Corruption

Harriet Kemp

Harriet Kemp was former head of engagement for the Institute of Business Ethics. She is currently head of ethics for Serco, an international information technology, consulting, and public services firm.

Making ethical decisions in the global marketplace is challenging for companies and their employees, but a culture of integrity begins with strong leadership. For the battle against bribery and corruption to be taken seriously, corporate leaders must maintain a zero-tolerance threshold for corruption and create an environment of transparency.

Bribery, corruption and facilitation payments were the most commonly reported issues recorded by the Institute of Business Ethics' media monitoring during 2013. They accounted for 13% of all the stories on business ethics. The sectors most frequently mentioned were extractives (70%), defence and security (63%), pharmaceuticals (47%) and broadcast/media (33%).

Businesses still have some way to go to embed anti-bribery and corruption mechanisms effectively into their culture. This gap between saying and doing is also reflected in external studies. A survey by Control Risks and the Economist Intelligence Unit found that 25% of companies felt there was at least a "somewhat likely chance" their company would be required to investigate a suspected violation of anti-bribery laws involving an employee in the next two years.

The Cost of Corruption

The effects of corruption on society are well documented. Politically it represents an obstacle to democracy and the rule of law; economically it depletes a country's wealth, often diverting it to corrupt officials' pockets and, at its core, it puts an imbalance in the way that business is done, enabling those who practise corruption to win.

> *Employers need to provide relevant support to staff to help them recognise, understand and respond to the ethical challenges they may face.*

The language of bribery also deceives, implying that what is being offered or expected is of no consequence. But corruption is not a victimless crime; it leads to decisions being made for the wrong reasons. Contracts are awarded because of kickbacks and not whether they are the best value for the community. Corruption costs people freedom, health and human rights and, in the worst cases, their lives. It may also cost companies, as the UK [United Kingdom] Anti-Bribery Act takes force, making an organisation culpable if it fails to have "adequate procedures" in place to stop bribery and corruption.

The Challenge for Companies

Most companies offer employees some guidance on anti-bribery and corruption. However, the global nature of today's business means that organisations can have difficulties when trying to embed policies around the globe.

[Former chairman of the Communist Party of China] Mao Zedong said "food before ethics". While no one would suggest that bribery and corruption are good things, if you believe your job is dependent on offering or paying a bribe, the corruption policy sent round by head office may have little bearing on your decision in the moment.

Employers need to provide relevant support to staff to help them recognise, understand and respond to the ethical challenges they may face.

Creating a culture that influences employees' actions, decision making and behaviour can be a challenging and lengthy process, requiring sensitivity, patience and resources. Corruption can be so ingrained into a company's culture as to be considered "the way business is done".

This can be the case especially for companies who use agents, or who operate in countries where enforcement of anti-corruption regulation is poor and facilitation payments are seen as the norm. Getting staff to see that a backhander is actually a form of corruption takes time and requires regular communication and training.

Support for Staff

Difficult decisions for employees often arise in everyday situations, when travelling, when offering or accepting gifts and hospitality or when negotiating with customers and suppliers. Anyone can offer or be offered a bribe. Being clear about what can and can't be accepted is good business practice and reduces the risk of corruption.

The Institute of Business Ethics has developed a free app, the Say No toolkit, which provides the practical guidance to recognise a difficult situation and to do the right thing in response. It has been designed to help employees have the confidence to make the right decision in situations which could lead to accusations of bribery.

Tone at the Top

But even with the support of decision-making tools and apps, it is one thing to know the "right" decision to make, but often another to be able to apply that decision. Factors such as fear, ignorance, and real or perceived pressure to meet business targets, or pressure from a more senior figure, can make ethical decision-making harder.

Visible support from leadership is critical; the impact of leading by example should not be underestimated. If senior management declare a zero-tolerance approach to bribery and corruption, they must demonstrate that they will support staff if they lose contracts or business in the short-term as a result. Creating a culture of integrity and openness—where ethical dilemmas arising from doing business in corruption hotspots are discussed, and employees feel supported to do the right thing—is a powerful way to help mitigate against the risk of an ethical lapse.

The culture of an organisation is ultimately set by people at the top. Leaders who regularly talk about ethical issues, support staff to uphold ethical standards and behave in an open and transparent way send the message to all employees, and to the wider world, that the fight against corruption is taken seriously.

3

Corporate Executives Should Be Paid Less

Margaret Heffernan

Margaret Heffernan is a former chief executive officer and entrepreneur as well as an award-winning author of several business and finance books, including A Bigger Prize *and* Beyond Measure: The Big Impact of Small Changes.

Excessive executive compensation not only isolates corporate leaders from those in their employ but also breeds an attitude of arrogance and entitlement. True leaders should be willing to sacrifice large salaries and exorbitant bonuses for the benefit of their corporate and social community—those they were hired to serve.

When David Winters, a longtime money manager, read the Coca-Cola Company's annual report recently, the amount of stock put aside to reward the company's managers stopped him in his tracks. Over the next four years, some $13 billion of stock was set aside for company executives. This would have meant that fully 14.2 percent of company stock was being used to motivate a management team already well paid. According to the *New York Times*, Winters argued that "it is unfathomable that they would require such astronomical sums of money to provide motivation."

It isn't just unfathomable. It's wrong. Why?

Why Money Is Not the Best Motivator

First of all, money isn't a great motivator. While it may offer temporary delight, its value soon wears off. We all accommodate to what we get, so its value as a long-term incentive is slight.

Companies that pay excessively isolate themselves and their executives from the societies they ostensibly exist to serve.

Moreover, money inhibits our sense of social connectedness. In a series of intriguing experiments, students were asked to play Monopoly. When they were done and leaving the lab, an assistant crossed the room and spilled a box of pencils. Here was the focus of the experiment: Which students would prove most helpful? The ones who had made the least amount of money in the game. All over the world, there have been any number of permutations of this kind of research—some in labs, some in the real world—and they all point relentlessly to the same conclusion: Money cuts people off from one another.

This isn't really so remarkable. When I fly in a private jet, drive in a limousine, stay in luxury hotels where my every need is catered for—all things I have done at some stage—at first this is all delightful. Then it's normal. Then it's an entitlement. I've watched this happen—to me and to others. The luxury has corroded my sense of self as normal, imperfect, just like everyone else. If I believe the money, then I imagine I am better, different and separate from other people.

Moreover, geographically the money also separates me from everyone else. On private planes I don't have to sit next to crying babies. Eschewing public transportation, I don't have any sense of public mood or morale. Behind tall gates, my home provides splendid isolation.

All of this is exactly what you do not want in managers who are supposed to be connected to their market and their workforce. It's a recipe for arrogance, not motivation. Or, as Anthony Salz wrote, when investigating the manipulation of LIBOR [London InterBank Offered Rates: the average inter-bank interest rate at which a selection of banks on the London money market charge each other for short term loans] rates at Barclays Bank, "Elevated pay levels inevitably distort culture, tending to attract people who measure their personal success principally on compensation. . . . Many interviewees [reported] a sense of an entitlement culture." Companies that pay excessively isolate themselves and their executives from the societies they ostensibly exist to serve.

Excessive Pay for Talent Is the Wrong Approach

The old argument—that you have to pay to secure real talent—is exactly wrong. If you have to pay to get or keep your talent, you end up with the wrong person. Consider instead the view of Charles Munger of Berkshire Hathaway: "People should take way less than they're worth when they're favored by life," he says, further arguing that when you have risen high enough, you have a "moral duty to be underpaid—not to get all you can, but to actually be underpaid."

And Munger stood by his belief, resolutely paying the CEO [chief executive officer] of Costco (a Berkshire Hathaway investment) less (in cash and stock) than his peers were paid running Walmart, Home Depot or Target. Since Berkshire Hathaway is a big investor in Coca-Cola, it will be interesting to see how it responds to the stock allocation that has so riled David Winters.

Exorbitant pay isn't—or shouldn't be—news. That it continues to be so can only be explained by one thing, as one senior executive commented to me recently: Everyone hopes somebody else will go first—and reduce pay. All the boards want to. Most of the CEOs want to. They all know it needs to happen. But no one wants to be first. You could call it the biggest game of chicken the world has ever seen.

Wall Street Executives Deserve Their Big Bonuses

Alan Pyke

Alan Pyke is deputy economic policy editor for ThinkProgress .org, a liberal political website published by the Center for American Progress.

Although the chief executive officers of several megabanks received strong criticism for earning large raises in the wake of the financial collapse and government bailout, they were each successful in chartering their corporations back to financial viability and thus deserve to be financially rewarded.

Three of the country's largest financial companies are giving their CEOs [chief executive officers] huge raises for 2013, complete with large stock packages. Despite the outrage those raises have prompted, the three men more than earned those pay bumps by sidestepping major legal and financial consequences for their contributions to the financial crisis.

Lloyd Blankfein, CEO of Goldman Sachs, is getting paid $23 million for 2013, a roughly 10 percent raise despite a flat year of revenues and steep drops in trading income from some of its core businesses, the company announced this week [January 2014]. Earlier this month JP Morgan's board revealed that it is paying CEO Jamie Dimon 74 percent more than it did for 2012, and might throw him another $34 million later this year. Morgan Stanley CEO James Gorman is getting an 88 percent bump to his stock options, although his total compensation isn't yet known. The government is subsidizing all three of these big pay raises thanks to a loophole in the tax code.

Why Large Bonuses Make Sense

Dimon's raise brought the most heated criticism, but it is also perhaps the best example of how different things look from the perspective of financial company boardrooms than from Main Street. JP Morgan made headlines for paying the largest government legal settlement in U.S. history, critics of Dimon's raise say, and failed to post a new record annual profit for the first time since 2009. But considering that the government had strong enough evidence on the bank that it was prepared to go to court—a highly unusual move for Attorney General Eric Holder—the deal Dimon struck is a very good one from JP Morgan's perspective. Furthermore, as ThinkProgress has detailed repeatedly, the deal won't actually cost the bank the $13 billion that Holder and others have claimed. After tax deductions and some fine print in the deal, it will really only cost the company something like $5 billion. The company's stock rose 33 percent last year and Jamie Dimon outfoxed the feds, so why *shouldn't* he get a 74 percent raise?

Rather than attacking individual companies' decisions, critics would do well to train their fire on the broken system of rules governing executive compensation.

Gorman, the Morgan Stanley chief executive, stands to make a lot more money than he did last year even though he led the bank to an earnings performance "that is roughly half of Gorman's stated target" by one key measure, according to Reuters. So how could he get a raise? Morgan Stanley has been the most successful of all banks at avoiding legal and financial consequences for its financial crisis activities. Leading the industry in penalty avoidance is worth a lot, apparently.

Blankfein can make a similar case. Considering that the firm is now under investigation for its role in controlling the price of aluminum, and that one of its employees was on trial this year for designing a brazen form of deception that made Goldman Sachs a great deal of money in the run-up to the financial collapse, the firm has gotten away relatively unscathed. A lawsuit tied to Goldman's allegedly fraudulent crisis-era deals was dismissed in early 2013, and responsibility for the company's actions in that deal is falling on one individual's shoulders.

Blame Rules Governing Executive Compensation

The biggest banks and financial firms have bounced back to near-record profitability in just a few short years. The crisis they caused ripped at least $6 trillion, and perhaps more like $20 trillion, out of the economy. Next to all that damage, the legal bills those companies have faced are minuscule, and the heads of those companies are being rewarded for that victory.

The individual outrages tied to each bank's recent actions conceal the core reality of the financial industry. These three men successfully minimized the legal and financial damage from deals relating to the financial crisis and brought huge stock price returns to their shareholders. The financial system is designed to reward that behavior handsomely. Rather than attacking individual companies' decisions, critics would do well to train their fire on the broken system of rules governing executive compensation.

Globalization Has Benefitted Corporations but Hurt Workers

Robert McGarvey

Robert McGarvey is an economic historian, cofounder of the Genuine Wealth Institute, and author of The Creative Revolution, *which discusses economics and modern capitalism.*

International trade treaties of the last century were designed to create a profitable future for both corporations and global citizens. However, globalization initiatives and free trade agreements have harmed societies but continue to benefit corporations, whose reach and power extend beyond international borders and into politics, holding sway over issues they deem threatening to their own interests.

Cordell Hull, the crusty U.S. Secretary of State during the Second World War was very clear about the causes of war: "*Unhampered trade dovetailed with peace, high tariffs, trade barriers, and unfair economic competition, with war*".

He, for one, was determined to reform the global economy at war's end.

As the tide slowly turned against Nazi Germany in the autumn of 1943, Hull and other world leaders began to turn their attention to the future. In July of '44, almost a year before the end of hostilities, the Allied nations (minus the

Soviets) gathered together at Bretton Woods in New Hampshire to design a new and better world.

Brazilian representative Arthur de Souza Costa spoke for many when in his opening address, he outlined the lofty goals of the conference: It (Bretton Woods Conference) *"is inspired by a single ideal—that happiness be distributed throughout the face of the earth."*

Globalization Began with High Ideals

The principal architects of the Conference, British economist John Maynard Keynes and Cordell Hull, wrestled with problems that had plagued the global economy for ages: protectionism versus free trade, universalism versus regionalism, non-discrimination versus preferential arrangements.

They were also inspired with a bold vision 'to reconcile liberal international trade policies with high levels of domestic employment and growth'. Their larger goal: 'to devise an international system benefiting not just the world community as a whole, but each of its parts.'

The monetary and currency accords that were adopted at Bretton Woods helped launch a 'freer trading' post war world. As a result, globalization got off to a pretty good start.

While 'free trade' deals have created a borderless world for corporations, their goods and their money, globalization has basically hung workers of the world out to dry.

The Treaty of Paris (1951) established the European Coal and Steel Community, and in the process set an important standard in European cooperation. This was soon followed by the Treaty of Rome (1957), which established the European Atomic Energy Community.

With the success of these early supranational agreements, the road was cleared for more globalization initiatives, which accelerated the development of the European Economic Community, set the stage for the North American Free Trade Accords (NAFTA) and laid the foundations for the founding of the World Trade Organization.

It is a measure of how far we have fallen from those lofty ideals that—70 years later—globalization is increasingly labelled as a corporate boondoggle, a 'race to the bottom' for wages and working conditions, and an open license for environmental degradation.

While 'free trade' deals have created a borderless world for corporations, their goods and their money, globalization has basically hung workers of the world out to dry.

Globalization's 'creative destruction' has impacted everyone. Whole sectors of the Western economy have vanished as globalization centralizes industrial production in low-wage nations like China or Bangladesh. Meanwhile, globalization gets blamed for stagnant middle class wages, high levels of unemployment and everything from the European financial crisis to the need for fiscal austerity.

What happened to globalization and its high ideals?

You can draw a line in the historical sand, almost pinpoint the date when globalization ceased being broadly popular and became crudely self-serving.

Ironically, it was the fall of Soviet communism that tipped the balance.

With the tumbling of the Berlin Wall, the 'evil empire' of the Soviet Union disappeared, and with it went the need to strengthen the Free World, to tie globalization's outcomes to improving the lot of the general population.

In fact, the Free World as an idea was dropped altogether, when it became popular to believe the End of History had cemented liberal capitalism as the undisputed champion in the historical sweepstakes. From that point onward, it was no longer necessary to consciously raise the poor: victorious capitalism would do the job automatically if we just left it alone.

In the 1990's, the Washington Consensus and the IMF (International Monetary Fund) launched a new era, with its new idea of 'market purity' applying a new set of rules to globalization. From that point onward, corporations gained the upper hand. They could (and did) sue governments that threatened their free market interests by strengthening workers' rights, setting environmental standards or raising taxes.

Globalization Led to Corporatism "Unchained"

The result was corporatism 'unchained', a development that launched globalization on the road to its present condition.

We've lost a lot in the process, including the moral high ground. Westerners, for instance, no longer criticize the communist government of China for its flagrant human rights abuses. Why? Because we are all now party to those abuses through our involvement in the globalized economy.

Globalization is an unstoppable force, but if we are to share equally in its benefits, we need to recover some of the original idealism and create a more just and progressive global system.

Global Corporations Are More Powerful than Many Governments

Andrew Gavin Marshall

Andrew Gavin Marshall is a freelance writer based in Montreal, Canada. He is the director of Occupy.com's global power project and is also head of geopolitics for the Hampton Institute, a think tank dedicated to social change.

Some of the world's most profitable corporations are larger than most nations and as such pose a serious threat to the well-being of the global economy. They are totalitarian regimes that act as independent "supra-governments" and have no democratic accountability but hold huge sway over financial markets and the world economy.

We live in a corporate culture, where most of us have worked or currently work for corporations, we spend our money at corporate venues, on corporate products, watch corporately-owned television shows and movies, listen to corporate-sponsored music; our modes of transportation, communication and recreation are corporately influenced or produced; our sports stadiums and movie theaters are named after car companies and global banks; our food is genetically altered by multinational conglomerates, our drinking water is

Andrew Gavin Marshall, "Welcome to the Network of Global Corporate 'Supra-Government'," Truthout, February 7, 2013, www.occupy.com. Copyright © 2013 Occupy.com. All rights reserved. Reproduced with permission.

brought to us by Coca-Cola, our news is brought to us by Pfizer, and our political leaders are brought to us by Exxon, Shell, Goldman Sachs and JP Morgan Chase.

In this global corporate culture it is often difficult to take a step back and look at transnational corporations, beyond what they represent in our culture, and see that they are, in fact, totalitarian institutions with power being exercised from the top down, with no democratic accountability, legally bound to be interested only—and exclusively—in maximizing quarterly short-term profits, often to the detriment of the environment, labor, human rights, democracy, peace and the population as a whole.

In the year 2000, of the world's 100 largest economies, 51 were corporations, while only 49 were countries, based upon national GDP (gross domestic product) and corporate sales.

In this first of a three-part series on the reaches of global corporate power, we'll look specifically at the size and network influence of the world's largest corporations. This is especially important given that the world's population faces increasing challenges with over 1 billion people living in slums, billions more living in poverty, hunger and increasing starvation; with unemployment increasing, austerity and "adjustment" programs demanding that even those in the once-industrialized West dramatically reduce their living standards; as the environment is plundered and pillaged, and as governments give corporations more state welfare and subsidies while cutting welfare and social services for the poor.

Corporate culture creates, over time, a totalitarian culture as this dominant institution seeks to remake society in its own image—where people are punished and impoverished as corporations are supported, rewarded and empowered.

The Network of Global Corporate Control, in Numbers

In the year 2000, of the world's 100 largest economies, 51 were corporations, while only 49 were countries, based upon national GDP (gross domestic product) and corporate sales. Of the top 200 corporations in 2000, the United States had the largest share with 82, followed by Japan at 41, Germany at 20, and France at 17.

Of the world's 100 largest economic entities in 2010, 42% were corporations; when looking at the top 150 economic entities, 58% were corporations. The largest corporation in 2010 was Wal-Mart, the 25th largest economic entity on earth, surpassed only by the 24 largest countries in the world, but with greater revenues than the GDP of 171 countries, placing it higher on the list than Norway and Iran.

Following Wal-Mart, the largest corporations in the world were: Royal Dutch Shell (larger than Austria, Argentina and South Africa), Exxon Mobil (larger than Thailand and Denmark), BP (larger than Greece, UAE, Venezuela and Colombia), followed by several other energy and automotive conglomerates.

In 2012, *Fortune* published its annual Global 500 list of the top 500 corporations in the world in 2011. The top 10 corporations in the world, as determined by total revenue, are: Royal Dutch Shell, Exxon Mobil, Wal-Mart Stores, BP, Sinopec Group, China National Petroleum, State Grid, Chevron, ConocoPhillips, and Toyota Motor.

Among some of the other top 100 are: Total (11), Gazprom (15), E.ON (16), ENI (17), ING Group (18), GM (19), General Electric (22), AXA (25), BNP Paribas (30), GDF Suez (33), Banco Santander (44), Bank of America (46), JP Morgan Chase (51), HSBC Holdings (53), Apple (55), IBM (57), Citigroup (60), Société Générale (67), Nestlé (71), Wells Fargo (80), Archer Daniels Midland (92), and Bank of China (93).

The 10 largest corporations in Canada include: Manulife Financial, Suncor Energy, Royal Bank of Canada, Power Corporation of Canada, George Weston, Magna International, Toronto-Dominion Bank, Bank of Nova Scotia, Onex, and Husky Energy.

The 10 largest corporations in Britain are: BP, HSBC Holdings, Tesco, Vodafone, Barclays, Lloyds Banking Group, Royal Bank of Scotland, Aviva, Rio Tinto Group, and Prudential.

The 10 largest conglomerates in France are: Total, AXA, BNP Paribas, GDF Suez, Carrefour, Crédit Agricole, Société Générale, Électricité de France, Peugeot, and Groupe BPCE.

An analysis of the relationships between 43,000 transnational corporations has identified a relatively small group of companies, mainly banks, with disproportionate power over the global economy.

The 10 largest conglomerates in Germany are: Volkswagen, E. ON, Daimler, Allianz, Siemens, BASF, BMW, Metro, Munich Re Group, and Deutsche Telekom.

The 10 largest conglomerates in the United States are: Exxon Mobil, Wal-Mart Stores, Chevron, ConocoPhillips, General Motors, General Electric, Berkshire Hathaway, Fannie Mae, Ford Motor, and Hewlett-Packard.

A Small Number of Companies Control the Global Economy

In October of 2011, a scientific study about the global financial system was released, the first of its kind, undertaken by three complex systems theorists at the Swiss Federal Institute of Technology in Zurich, Switzerland. The conclusion of the study revealed what many theorists and observers have noted for years:

"An analysis of the relationships between 43,000 transnational corporations has identified a relatively small group of companies, mainly banks, with disproportionate power over the global economy." As one of the researchers stated, "Reality is so complex, we must move away from dogma, whether it's conspiracy theories or free-market. . . . Our analysis is reality-based." Using a database which listed 37 million companies and investors worldwide, the researchers studied all 43,060 transnational corporations (TNCs), including the share ownerships linking them.

The mapping of "power" was done through the construction of a model showing which companies controlled other companies through shareholdings. The web of ownership revealed a core of 1,318 companies with ties to two or more other companies. This "core" was found to own roughly 80% of global revenues for the entire set of 43,000 TNCs.

And then came what the researchers referred to as the "super-entity" of 147 tightly-knit companies, which all own each other, and collectively own 40% of the total wealth in the entire network. One of the researchers noted, "In effect, less than 1 per cent of the companies were able to control 40 per cent of the entire network."

Risk to the World Economy

This network poses a huge risk to the global economy, noted the researchers: "If one [company] suffers distress . . . this propagates." The study was undertaken with a data set established prior to the economic crisis, thus, as the financial crisis forced some banks to fail (such as Lehman Brothers) and others to merge (such as Merrill Lynch and Bank of America), the "super-entity" would now be even more connected, concentrated, and thus, dangerous for the economy.

The top 50 companies on the list of the "super-entity" included (as of 2007): Barclays Plc (1), Capital Group Companies Inc (2), FMR Corporation (3), AXA (4), State Street Corporation (5), JP Morgan Chase & Co. (6), UBS AG (9), Merrill Lynch & Co Inc (10), Deutsche Bank (12), Credit Suisse Group

(14), Bank of New York Mellon Corp (16), Goldman Sachs Group (18), Morgan Stanley (21), Société Générale (24), Bank of America Corporation (25), Lloyds TSB Group (26), Lehman Brothers Holdings (34), Sun Life Financial (35), ING Groep (41), BNP Paribas (46), and several others.

In December of 2011, Roger Altman, the former Deputy Secretary of the Treasury under the [Bill] Clinton administration, wrote an article for the *Financial Times* in which he explained that financial markets were "acting like a global supra-government," noting:

> They oust entrenched regimes where normal political processes could not do so. They force austerity, banking bailouts and other major policy changes. Their influence dwarfs multilateral institutions such as the International Monetary Fund. Indeed, leaving aside unusable nuclear weapons, they have become the most powerful force on earth.

Altman continued, explaining that when the power of this "global supra-government" is flexed, "the immediate impact on society can be painful—wider unemployment, for example, frequently results and governments fail." But of course, being a former top Treasury Department official, he went on to praise the "global supra-government," writing that, "the longer-term effects can be often transformative and positive."

Ominously, Altman concluded: "Whether this power is healthy or not is beside the point. It is permanent," and "there is no stopping the new policing role of the financial markets."

So, this small network of dominant global companies and banks, many of which are larger than most countries on earth, with no democratic accountability, are also acting independently as a type of "global supra-government" forcing even our dysfunctional and façade-like "democratic" governments to collapse if they do not do as "financial markets" say—such as the recent cases of democratically-elected governments in Greece and Italy whose officials were forced out and replaced with unelected bankers.

In any other situation that's called a coup d'état. But as Altman's view reflected, powerful government officials will not oppose this network, whether or not the power is good for human lives and human communities—which is, in Altman's words, "beside the point." After all, in his view, "it is permanent."

Unless, of course, the people of the world decide to have a say in the matter.

7

Global Corporations Profit from Climate Destruction

Philippa de Boissière et al.

The following viewpoint was written by Philippa de Boissière and six other authors. She is a postgraduate student at the University of Sussex, United Kingdom, specializing in climate change and policy.

Powerful multinational companies—Repsol, Glencore Xstrata, and Enel-Endesa—pretend to provide solutions for climate change when they are, in fact, the driving forces behind it. Their corruption extends beyond South American rainforests, where they extract natural resources, and reach deep into local communities to exploit workers as well as influence national politics.

Just at a time when the world is coming to understand how urgent it is to put the brakes on dirty energy, the fossil fuel industry, with Repsol as a leading actor, is methodically moving in exactly the opposite direction. Since its emergence onto the international scene in the late 1990s, the Spanish oil and gas giant has quickly risen to the major leagues of the global industry.

Among oil and gas corporations, Repsol is now investing in future reserves at one of the highest rates in the world (its reserve replacement ratio in 2013 was 275%—the highest in the business), including in some of the planet's most vulnerable locations, such as the Amazon rainforest.

What's more, the fossil fuels Repsol is targeting include some of the most destructive on the planet. Repsol has been busy upgrading capacity in its oil refineries in Spain in preparation for receiving Canadian tar sands oil. As well as decimating boreal forests and destroying indigenous territories in Canada, extracting from the tar sands is much more carbon intensive than conventional oil and gas. Their exploitation has been described by NASA [National Aeronautics and Space Administration] scientist James Hansen as "game over for the climate." Despite strong resistance, Europe's first major shipment of tar sands oil arrived at Repsol's Bilbao refinery in Spain in May 2014. All of this took place on the watch of then Spanish environment minister Miguel Arias Cañete, who also approved Repsol's controversial plans to drill in a UNESCO [United Nations Education, Scientific and Cultural Organization] world heritage site in the Canary Islands, yet is now European Commissioner for Climate and Energy.

It comes as no surprise then to see that Repsol was included as one of the top 90 corporations in the world most responsible for causing climate change in "Carbon Majors"—a groundbreaking peer-reviewed study published in the scientific journal *Climatic Change* in 2013.

Currently 75% of the Peruvian Amazon is covered by hydrocarbon concessions and Repsol is leading the charge to open up more Amazon rainforests to fossil fuel expansion.

In terms of economic and political power, Repsol also sits among the elites of the global fossil fuel industry. Over the past 25 years, Repsol has paid out more than €16 billion in dividends and its market value has increased by a multiple of 8.5. In 2013, the corporation had revenues of US$60 billion and operating profits of US$1,757 million. When it comes to political influence, as we'll see below, Repsol is at the centre of a network of European and international lobbying groups working around the clock to stop regulations that would threaten its bottom line.

While Repsol likes to flaunt its image as a "global company looking out for the well-being of all people" its record in social and environmental devastation, causing and exacerbating climate change, political meddling and creative accounting methods (twelve different tax havens appear in its annual accounts for year ending 2010) tell a different story.

Peru—Repsol's Attacks on the Rainforests and Indigenous Communities

After Brazil, Peru has the most forest cover in Latin America and the ninth most forest cover in the world. It is home to hundreds of indigenous communities and some of the most biodiverse areas of the planet. Currently 75% of the Peruvian Amazon is covered by hydrocarbon concessions and Repsol is leading the charge to open up more Amazon rainforests to fossil fuel expansion.

The most vivid example of what Repsol is up to in the region is the Camisea Gas Project—the largest and most controversial energy project in Peru. Camisea is located in the Vilcabamba mountain range and the lower Urubamba River, an area designated as one of twenty-five global "hotspots" for conservation due to its biological richness. The project involves the extraction of natural gas in the middle of this rainforest by means of dozens of drilling platforms, hundreds of kilometers of gas pipelines, recovery plants, ports, helipads, access roads and the installation of power lines.

Repsol is at the heart of the Camisea project. It operates Lot 57 and is a partner of the Camisea Consortium in Lots 56 and 88, together with Hunt Oil, SK Group, Pluspetrol, Sonatrach and Tecpetrol. All of these Lots overlap with the territories of local indigenous communities. In Lot 57 Repsol plans to inaugurate a gas compression plant inside its camp, which is gradually being converted into an industrial site and is located just a few metres from the houses and schools of Nuevo Mundo, a Machiguenga indigenous community.

Lots 56 and 57 are to be connected to Lots 58 and 88 through a network of pipelines crossing the Urubamba River and dozens of smaller tributaries. Meanwhile, the Malvinas plant, an extensive petro-chemical compound inside Lot 88, is being expanded to accommodate new production from Lot 57.

The indigenous people in the region have slowly been surrounded by an all-consuming mega-industrial complex.

One key impact of the Camisea Project is on the local environment. In the first years of the project the region saw some major spills. A succession of leaks in the gas-pipe from Camisea to Pisco [Peru] between 2004 and 2006 caused serious damage to river ecosystems and fish stocks.

As with the case of Glencore in Espinar [Peru], at a time when extreme weather due to climate change puts pressure on water sources through increasing droughts, flooding and glacier loss, corporate expansion in environmentally vulnerable areas is polluting fresh water supplies for local communities.

While Communal Reserves were established in order to protect the biodiversity and territories of the indigenous communities living in the area the seismic testing, building of drilling platforms and installation of wells and pipelines associated with Camisea have all meant intense deforestation and fragmentation of ecosystems. This deforestation, combined with water pollution and the new helicopter traffic in the area, is affecting the ability of local populations to fish and hunt, eroding their food sovereignty and autonomy.

The presence of the corporations also has severe impacts on the social fabric of the communities. Jobs with the corporations and their subsidiaries are mostly for non-qualified manual labour roles, some with harsh working conditions. The cash economy results in shifts in consumption patterns with increased reliance on imported processed food and availability of alcohol. According to Jackeline Binari from the Machiguenga Council of the Urubamba River, Camisea has brought with it severe changes in lifestyle "with impacts on diet and nutrition—with increased childhood malnutrition, increased domestic violence and alcohol consumption."

In more remote areas corporations are giving handouts and effectively buying off local opposition through the provision of sub-standard services in compensation for their projects. According to Peruvian lawyer Miluska Carhuavilca, "the company ends up establishing itself like a mini-State within the community . . . a relationship of dependence is established . . . and a time comes when the communities can't say no to the company, they fear that these things that they have a right to anyway—such as schools and health centres—are dependent on the presence of the company."

At the centre of a Peruvian minerals rush which is causing severe social and environmental conflicts looms the mining and commodities giant Glencore Xstrata.

Communities that have been self-sufficient for generations gradually lose their autonomy and become dependent on the "charity"—or blackmail—of transnational corporations. . . .

Repsol's Toxic Influence in Peruvian Politics

In order to maintain and expand its practices, Repsol has used various mechanisms to assert its influence on national policy in Peru over the years. Repsol is now a member of the Peruvian Hydrocarbons Society, a powerful industry lobby group which in early 2014 published its *White Book of Hydrocarbons*, laying out a wish list of changes to national environmental laws in favour of the oil and gas industry. According to José de Echave, former second in command at Peru's Ministry of Environment before he resigned in protest at measures to undermine and weaken the environment ministry in 2011, "the Peruvian Hydrocarbons Society was actively lobbying and proposing reforms in Peru, many of which were included in the '*paquetazo*.'" The *paquetazo* is a sweeping set of changes to environmental laws introduced by the government in 2014 that directly affect indigenous territorial rights.

A further demonstration of how Repsol benefits from this tight industry-politics nexus in Peru relates to Lot 76, another concession in the Peruvian Amazon. Lot 76 is headed by Hunt Oil in partnership with Repsol and PlusPetrol. Hunt Oil is a client of Laub & Quijandria, a law firm closely connected to Eleodoro Mayorga. One month after Mayorga took over as Peruvian Minister for Mining and Energy in 2014, permits for Hunt Oil and Repsol in Lot 76 were approved despite indigenous communities calling for an investigation into irregularities in the licensing processes and the lack of any consultation. . . .

Glencore Xstrata: Mining the Future of Peruvian Communities

Throughout its history Peru has witnessed several waves of foreign intervention by those looking to cash in on its mineral wealth. Today this hunt for natural resources continues, bringing with it environmental destruction and severe human rights violations. Just as climate change impacts begin to take hold in the Peruvian Andes, the expansion of ever more ambitious mining operations is putting extreme pressure on the most basic element of life: water. At the centre of a Peruvian minerals rush which is causing severe social and environmental conflicts looms the mining and commodities giant Glencore Xstrata.

Global Energy Commodities and Resources—or Glencore—is a multinational corporation of epic proportions dedicated to the sourcing and commercialisation of raw materials (metals, minerals, oil, coal, and agricultural products) from around the globe. In 2013 Glencore merged with Anglo-Swiss Xstrata, propelling it to third largest mining corporation in the world. The mega multinational now has a presence in more than 50 countries, covering all five continents. With more than US$232 billion in annual income, Glencore Xstrata breezed in at number 10 in 2014's Fortune Global 500, the list of the 500 biggest corporations in the world by revenue.

While Glencore Xstrata likes to position itself publicly as "one of the most responsible mining companies in the world," nothing could be further from the truth. On the ground, its operations are directly driving a number of conflicts related to environmental contamination and human rights violations in countries such as Zambia, the Democratic Republic of Congo, Bolivia and Colombia. Meanwhile, at the international level, Glencore Xstrata is actively pushing for the continued use of coal and fossil fuels which will only further exacerbate the impacts of climate change and aggravate conflict. To legitimise the aggressive expansion of its destructive business model, Glencore predicts a future in which global demand will see fossil fuels make up 75% of the world's energy mix by 2050. In other words: business as usual.

In order to protect and promote that vision, Glencore Xstrata has not only embedded itself in industry lobby groups at the national level in countries like Peru. It is also embroiled in an enormous global network of over 60 international lobbying organisations with the intention of capturing climate change policy spaces and processes at all levels.

Peru's Espinar Province and Its Mineral Riches

The province of Espinar, where Glencore Xstrata's Tintaya and Antapaccay mining projects are located, is in the department of Cusco, in the southern Peruvian Andes. The province has a population of over 60,000 people, mostly farmers. The one hundred plus lakes and four major river basins in the area— Salado, Cañipía, Tintaya and Colca—are the region's lifeblood.

The Espinar municipality began legal actions against Xstrata in relation to environmental abuses at the Tintaya mine, even going as far as to call for a halt to operations at their other mine in Antapaccay.

Xstrata assumed operation of the Tintaya mine in 2006. The copper and iron produced by Tintaya is destined, not to benefit local Peruvians, but to be exported to the global market. In 2012, after three decades of exploitation, Tintaya initiated a process of closure. In order to maintain its supply to global markets, Xstrata subsequently began ramping up activities in the nearby Antapaccay open-cast mine, 10 kilometres from Tintaya. Glencore Xstrata, owner and operator of both mines, has earmarked Antapaccay as part of its major expansion programme in Peru. The multinational expects production to hit an average of 160,000 tonnes per year during its initial phase of operation, with the lifecycle of the project as a whole estimated at 20 years.

Un-Conventional Strategy: Xstrata's Dirty Tactics in Espinar

Multinational mining corporations have a long history of fraught relations with the people of Espinar. Local communities, who have been reporting contamination resulting from mining activities for years, have made collective demands on the corporation to take responsibility for the damages it has caused. In 2003, the authorities of Espinar and representatives from the Tintaya mine, then owned by BHP Billiton, signed a Framework Convention. The Convention committed the mine operator to a process of environmental monitoring and to contributing 3% royalties to the provincial government. It also set out promises to create more jobs and observe human rights standards.

However, in 2009 local communities accused the new mine-operator, Xstrata, of flagrant violations of the convention. According to the human rights defender Jaime Borda, the community began to report dangerous levels of environmental contamination leading to miscarriages, deformations and death in local livestock. Communities also accused Xstrata of trying to infiltrate and divide social organisations, of media manipulation and interference in local politics.

Glencore Xstrata is emblematic of why a profit-fuelled corporation with deep vested interests in fossil fuels shouldn't be allowed anywhere near climate policy-makers at any level.

In 2011 and early 2012 local organisations stepped up the pressure, calling for an immediate investigation into the environmental and health impacts of the mine and for the terms of the Framework Convention to be rewritten in light of worsening pollution. Communities also demanded compensation for families directly impacted by the mine and for royalties to local government to be scaled up. At the same time, the Espinar municipality began legal actions against Xstrata in relation to environmental abuses at the Tintaya mine, even going as far as to call for a halt to operations at their other mine in Antapaccay. . . .

Glencore Xstrata's Meddling in Peruvian Politics

Similarly to Repsol, Glencore Xstrata has friends in Peru that help the corporation bend the ear of national government. It is a member of the National Association of Mining, Oil and Energy (FUENTE), one of the most powerful industry associations in the country, made up of both national and international mining interests. According to the Observatory of Mining Conflicts, FUENTE, along with the Hydrocarbon Society, launched an intense media campaign pushing for environmental deregulation in the run up to the approval of the "paquetazo"; or Law 30230. The campaign asserted that the Peruvian economy was "slowing down" as a consequence of excessive environmental and social regulations, and encouraged the government to create a 'climate of investment' that suited their interests.

Not satisfied with this, corporate interests continue to push for additional policy changes that would further deregulate the Peruvian economy. . . .

A Perfect Storm of Corporate Misconduct

When we combine Glencore Xstrata's web of influence at the international level with its human rights impacts on communities—like in Espinar—and its political manoeuvring at national level in Peru, what we get is a perfect storm of corporate misconduct. Just like the case of Repsol above, we have a powerful multinational expanding its contaminating and water-intensive operations into ever more vulnerable areas of the planet, just as communities begin to feel the impacts of climate change. All the while it is busily interfering in democratic decision-making spaces to ensure that climate and other policies don't impinge on its economic interests. Glencore Xstrata is emblematic of why a profit-fuelled corporation with deep vested interests in fossil fuels shouldn't be allowed anywhere near climate policy-makers at any level.

Enel-Endesa Damming Progress on Climate While Flooding Local Communities

Multinational corporations, such as the ones featured in this report, are not only directly contributing to climate change. They are also busy peddling false solutions to the crisis in order to safeguard and expand their business model. "Carbon neutral" mega hydroelectric projects represent one such false solution that is being pushed onto South America by the EU [European Union] and the UN [United Nations]. Enel-Endesa, the largest private electricity corporation operating in Latin America, is striving for dominance in this reinvigorated market.

A refusal to acknowledge the climate impacts of hydroelectric projects is playing out with devastating consequences in South America. Just as Peru's "paquetazo" is axing through regulation designed to protect people and the environment, countries throughout the continent are competing in a deadly race to the bottom to attract corporate "investment," largely concentrated in extractive industries. For Colombia that means, amongst other consequences, opening the gate wide to new large-scale hydroelectric infrastructure.

For the people of Huila [Columbia] the Quimbo dam is like a recurring nightmare.

Enel-Endesa's Quimbo Dam: A Masterclass in Corporate Impunity

Enel-Endesa, formed by the acquisition of Endesa by Enel Group in 2009, is a European energy utility giant with a global reach in over 40 countries, particularly in South America. While its business model in Europe is centred on burning coal and gas, in South America—where operations span Peru, Chile, Argentina, Colombia and Brazil—its main focus is the deployment of hydroelectric dams. The corporation positions itself as a "Colombian company" in South America, operating under the name of Emgesa. In reality, the Italo-Spanish multinational is scoping out new opportunities for growth against a background of European economic downturn. In 2014 the multinational's $4.3bn [billion] profits increased by a staggering 286% from the previous year.

Emgesa's flagship project in Colombia is the El Quimbo megadam in the Department of Huila, in the south of the country. The project has been marred by controversy since day one. In 2007 Emgesa got the go-ahead to build a 400MW [megawatt] capacity dam on the Magdalena River, the main waterway in the country and a sustainer of livelihoods for communities from North to South. The "Quimbo" hydroelectric project stands to generate 2,216GWh [gigawatt hour] per year over an estimated lifespan of 50 years, making it one of the largest infrastructure developments in the country. The official discourse on the project positions the dam as essential to Colombia's energy future. But Colombia is already producing a surplus of energy. And so in practice the dam, which is expected to come into operation in early 2015, is being built with the express intention of carrying the surplus energy straight out of the country along transmission lines to Ecuador, Panama and the rest of Central America. On top of this, what stays inside the borders is to be sold at low cost to feed big extractive industry projects, such as foreign-owned gold mines in Northern Colombia and even for climate-wrecking shale gas operations, such as those within Huila itself.

Mining-energy policy has become the main "development locomotive" of the current Colombian government. Through it, vast swathes of territories are being handed over to foreign investors to deepen extraction activities, increasing social and environmental conflicts across the country—as the Quimbo case so powerfully illustrates.

For the people of Huila the Quimbo dam is like a recurring nightmare. In 1997 Central Hidroeléctrica de Betania had submitted proposals to construct a dam at the very same location. Routine investigations into the impacts of the project, however, concluded that the social and environmental costs would far outweigh any stated benefits. The proposal was subsequently declared "unviable" by the Environment Ministry. El Quimbo appeared to be dead and buried.

Ten years later Emgesa breathed new life into the project in the form of a US$837 million dollar cash injection. El Quimbo was back. This time, the project was exempt from having to undergo the same basic viability assessments that it had previously so conclusively failed. Since its approval El Quimbo has been defined by a growing catalogue of irregularities and abuses: a severe lack of transparency; ongoing failures to conduct adequate impact assessments; evasion of responsibilities to affected communities—including, as we have seen with Repsol, very serious failures to consult. Emgesa's conduct throughout the process has revealed a barefaced contempt for Colombia's regulatory frameworks. . . .

Unravelling Enel-Endesa's Web of Climate Influence

Despite engaging in bullyboy tactics across South America, the Italo-Spanish energy giant still presents a caring image of sustainability and climate action through its slick public relations campaigns and greenwash. In order to ensure Enel-Endesa is allowed to do what it does best—burn coal and gas and build socially and environmentally destructive megadams in South America—Enel and co. deploy a sprawling lobbying operation both at national and international levels. . . .

Enel-Endesa's Big Hydroelectric Climate Racket

While Enel is burning coal and dashing for (fracked) gas in Europe, in South America it is taking advantage of the opportunities presented by lucrative hydroelectric projects such as "El Quimbo" in Huila, Colombia. The energy being generated by these megaprojects is not providing low carbon "development" for South Americans. Rather they are high in emissions and provide cheap energy to ramp up fossil fuel extraction elsewhere. Engaging in hydroelectric projects (and CCS [carbon capture and storage]) provides a profitable green veneer for the company, allowing it to earn carbon offsets for its European business, while trampling on human and environmental rights overseas. Big Hydroelectric is not a "clean alternative," it is a highly damaging industry featuring all the same players as the supposedly "dirtier" fossil fuel industry. Set against the context of Enel's lobbying strategy—slashing away at regulations that may impede their profits on the one hand, while capturing climate research and policy agendas with the other—it's clear that the multinational's political tricks are as dirty as their business activities.

8

Corporate Profiteering
Is the Source of
Environmental Violence

Chris Williams

Chris Williams, author of Ecology and Socialism: Solutions to Capitalist Ecological Crisis, *is department chair of science for Packer Collegiate Institute. He also teaches in the department of chemistry and physical science at Pace University.*

The nature of capitalism is to value individual needs over the community. Corporations, specifically, prioritize their own profit and wealth above social welfare. Most often, environmental violence—such as global climate change and pollution—is the by-product of a corrupt capitalist system.

Both the words "environment" and "violence" have so many meanings, that they require some definition of how they can be of use in the context of a struggle for social justice. Regarding the word violence, according to Merriam Webster, one definition is "the use of brute strength to cause harm to a person or property"; a definition that doesn't seem to have an immediately obvious connection to ecological issues associated with climate change, loss of biodiversity and various forms of pollution.

"Ecology" Rather than "Environment"

An increasing number of environmental activists, myself included, regard the word "environment" with some suspicion, generally preferring the term "ecological." The reasoning behind the change in emphasis is because using the word "environment" posits the idea that nature is something that surrounds humans, but at the same time, something that we are fundamentally outside of, and separate from. The separation of nature from humans is the ideological position underlying capitalist orthodoxy; namely that the biosphere is a subset of the economy, rather than the other way around. Capitalists can freely take "natural resources" from outside of the economy as inputs, and dump waste from the production process back into the environment as outputs. Mainstream economic theory then pronounces that the ramifications of such an outlook will have only limited impact on the planet as a whole, and, thereby, economic accumulation and growth can continue indefinitely.

Exploitation of the natural world, driven forward by the never-ending hunt for profits, is merely the flip side of the exploitation of humans, put to work to turn the source of sustenance into money.

"Ecological," on the other hand, embeds humans back within the external world as a natural component of it, the same as any other organism. The use of tools such as microscopes, or Magnetic Resonance Imaging devices, can then be seen not simply as humans investigating nature in order to understand it, but that we are concurrently investigating ourselves, because tools are merely mechanical extensions of our bodily senses. No doubt, [German philosopher and economist Karl] Marx would very much approve of such an attention to the hidden social meaning of words, particularly with regard, in this example, to his very important concept of "metabolic rift": the devastating and unnatural split or break between humans and nature, forced on us by capitalist social relations.

Given these issues, and the importance of words to explain and communicate thought, how should those of us engaged in a struggle against capitalist environmental violence, conceive of that fight? If we are to argue that the social, economic and political system known as capitalism is the root cause of environmental violence, what are we arguing it is responsible for?

Interestingly enough, but, perhaps unsurprisingly given the prevalence of overt violence in our world, the dictionary gives almost 50 related words for "violence." These begin with words such as "coercion," "compulsion," "constraint," go on to "barbarity," "brutality," "damage" and continue with "onslaught," "tumult" and "upheaval."

Putting these words into a human context and joining them up with the word "environment" now starts to make significant sense. It is no longer possible to restrict violence to an act that is immediate and causes direct and obvious harm, whether that is in the most commonly thought of cases of warfare, police brutality, or state-sponsored torture such as waterboarding, or racist, sexist or homophobic language and bigotry.

The Meaning of Environmental Violence

Capitalist environmental violence rests on the dual exploitation of humans and nature, which were regarded by Marx as the twin sources of all wealth. Exploitation of the natural world, driven forward by the never-ending hunt for profits, is merely the flip side of the exploitation of humans, put to work to turn the source of sustenance into money. Viewed this way, socialists fighting for social justice and a different world cannot avoid integrating a fight for ecological justice, as the two are inseparable components of the same fight.

In this broadened understanding of violence, capitalism is an intensely violent system, as it depends on the systematic coercion of workers who are daily faced with the choice of working for "a living" or starvation and homelessness; their life choices for education, health and human fulfillment are hugely constrained by the unyielding ferocity of class exploitation and racism. Billions of people's lives are stunted and foreshortened by the daily violence meted out to them via the dictates of a system that prioritizes profit above all else. In Volume I of *Capital*, Marx's words resonate as much in our day as his:

> In its blind unrestrainable passion, its werewolf hunger for surplus-labour, capital oversteps not only the moral, but even the merely physical maximum bounds of the working-day. It usurps the time for growth, development, and healthy maintenance of the body. It steals the time required for the consumption of fresh air and sunlight. It higgles over a meal-time, incorporating it where possible with the process of production itself, so that food is supplied to the labourer as to a mere means of production, as coal is supplied to the boiler, grease and oil to the machinery. It reduces the sound sleep needed for the restoration, reparation, refreshment of the bodily powers to just so many hours of torpor as the revival of an organism, absolutely exhausted, renders essential.

But for Marx, the violent treatment of humans by capitalist social relations, in shortening and hamstringing their lives through overwork, poor housing, inadequate food and pollution, was directly analogous to capitalist farming practices:

> Capital cares nothing for the length of labour-power. All that concerns it is simply and solely the maximum of labour-power that can be rendered fluent in a working-day. It attains this end by shortening the extent of the [worker's] life, as a greedy farmer snatches increased produce from the soil by robbing it of its fertility.

One can only have nutritious food, health care, or decent housing located in an unpolluted neighborhood, if one has the money to pay for those things. Lack of access to these necessities by some, where others have access, makes the violence explicit. Furthermore, there is the violence of institutionalized racism, and a culture saturated with sexism that turns women's bodies into objects, doubly exploits them through unpaid domestic labor, and in the United States, refuses to allow women control over their own reproductive organs.

The Social Alienation of the Working Class

There is the associated psychological violence done to humans against our own sociality, whereby we are forced to live, in Marx's emotive phrase, in "dot-like isolation," as the primacy of the individual over the collective is sanctified. Few have written of the social alienation and environmental degradation suffered by working people with greater effect than [German social scientist] Frederick Engels, in his classic study, *The Condition of the Working Class in England.*

From the Ogoni people in Nigeria fighting Shell, to indigenous people poisoned by Chevron in the forests of Ecuador, the paramilitary arm of the state serves corporate priorities the world over.

Engels highlights the contradiction engendered by capitalism, between bringing millions of people together in giant urban conglomerations, which, rather than fostering collective solidarity and companionship, instead produce its opposite—an unfeeling and solitary individuality that corrupts the human spirit:

After roaming the streets of the capital a day or two, making headway with difficulty through the human turmoil and the endless lines of vehicles, after visiting the slums of the metropolis, one realises for the first time that these Londoners have been forced to sacrifice the best qualities of their human nature, to bring to pass all the marvels of civilisation which crowd their city; that a hundred powers which slumbered within them have remained inactive, have been suppressed in order that a few might be developed more fully and multiply through union with those of others.

For Engels, this produces feelings and a mode of living that is profoundly alienating of all that is good about humans:

> The brutal indifference, the unfeeling isolation of each in his private interest, becomes the more repellent and offensive, the more these individuals are crowded together, within a limited space. And, however much one may be aware that this isolation of the individual, this narrow self-seeking, is the fundamental principle of our society everywhere, it is nowhere so shamelessly barefaced, so self-conscious as just here in the crowding of the great city. The dissolution of mankind into monads, of which each one has a separate principle, the world of atoms, is here carried out to its utmost extreme.

Of course, there is the more overt and immediate violence of the state against people trying to protect their land from environmental degradation and ensuing displacement and poverty associated with fossil fuel extraction. From the Ogoni people in Nigeria fighting Shell, to indigenous people poisoned by Chevron in the forests of Ecuador, the paramilitary arm of the state serves corporate priorities the world over.

Environmental Violence Plays Out in Myriad Ways

In North America, this was brutally demonstrated in September [2013], as members of the Elsipogtog Mi'kmaq First Nation, alongside local residents, blockaded a road in New Brunswick, Canada. They were trying to prevent fracking exploration and were assaulted and tear gassed for their protest by paramilitary police.

The group, which had never been asked about whether they wanted their land used in this way, had blocked the road to stop shale gas exploration by SWN Resources Canada, a subsidiary of the Houston-based Southwestern Energy Co. As Susan Levi-Peters, the former chief of the nearby Elsipogtog indigenous group, told reporters, "The RCMP [Royal Canadian Mounted Police] is coming in here with their tear gas— they even had dogs on us. . . . They were acting like we're standing there with weapons, while we are standing there, as women, with drums and eagle feathers."

There are myriad ways in which environmental violence plays out, especially when it is compounded by climate change. So, for example, in Sub-Saharan Africa, lack of tree-cover from ongoing deforestation, means even when rain comes, it runs off the land and carries fertile topsoil with it. As a result, women and girls, who are responsible for over 70 percent of water collection, have to travel further and further to obtain it. The UN [United Nations] estimates that women in Sub-Saharan Africa spend 200 million hours per day collecting water for food and farming purposes, or 40 billion hours annually.

In 1992, Lawrence Summers, who was at the time chief economist of the World Bank, later to become [former US president] Bill Clinton's Treasury Secretary, president of Harvard, and most recently one of [Barack] Obama's key economic advisors in his first cabinet, wrote in an internal World Bank memorandum published by *The Economist*:

"Just between you and me, shouldn't the World Bank be encouraging more migration of the dirty industries to the LDCs [least developed countries]?" By way of answering his own question, he gives three reasons. Here's the first:

(1) The measurement of the costs of health-impairing pollution depends on the forgone earnings from increased morbidity and mortality. From this point of view a given amount of health-impairing pollution should be done in the country with the lowest cost, which will be the country with the lowest wages. I think the economic logic behind dumping a

load of toxic waste in the lowest-wage country is impeccable and we should face up to that.

The fact that a major establishment actor is able to advocate and rationalize the dumping of toxic waste on poor communities is a perfect illustration of the inhumanity of the thought process behind capitalist decision-making.

The unplanned, shorter and shorter time frames upon which capitalism operates, clash with the longer and longer term effects of the actions taken on those shorter time scales.

As I have argued, we need a much broader definition of violence than is allowed for by limiting its meaning to a physical and immediate brutal act of aggression, and one that includes an environmental dimension. Violence can happen over extended periods of time. Exploited workers in unhealthy conditions and poor communities exposed to toxins gradually succumb to a worsening quality of life, through a compendium of often intersecting long-term ailments. Due to financial restrictions on health care (itself a violent act), they often can't treat these illnesses by going to the doctor, seeking another job, or relocating to a different neighborhood.

A broadened definition of violence is exactly what Rob Nixon, Rachel Carson Professor of English at the University of Madison, argues is required in his book, *Slow Violence and the Environmentalism of the Poor*:

By slow violence I mean a violence that occurs gradually and out of sight, a violence of delayed destruction that is dispersed across time and space, an attritional violence that is typically not viewed as violence at all. Violence is customarily conceived as an event or action that is immediate in time, explosive and spectacular in space, and as erupting in sensational visibility.

That is to say, the unplanned, shorter and shorter time frames upon which capitalism operates, clash with the longer and longer term effects of the actions taken on those shorter time scales. Human induced climate change is arguably the primary and perfect example of just such a contradiction between the short-term priorities of capitalism to make profit from continuing to burn fossil fuels, and the longer term implications for future generations of humans, and planetary life in general, due to the now well-known side-effect of increased concentrations of atmospheric carbon dioxide. One could reasonably debate whether climate change, or the irradiation of the atmosphere from atomic tests and the need to deal with nuclear waste from nuclear power plants—waste that remains toxic and deadly for hundreds of thousands of years—is a more disruptive and long-term negative impact of capitalist social relations.

A Democracy Based on Cooperation

In the more immediate sense, while we currently produce enough food to feed everyone on the planet, over one billion people suffer starvation and hunger. In discussing why people starve in England, when food was in fact abundant, Engels posed the question of who should be blamed for the extreme violence of death by starvation: "The English working-men call this 'social murder', and accuse our whole society of perpetrating this crime perpetually. Are they wrong?"

In answering Engels' question, one must blame the system for the long-term "social murder" of our planet, and the daily degradation and violence of life under capitalism. Given the critical state of the biosphere and an exploitative and constantly-growing economic model based on profit and fossil fuels for energy, which is bringing about global climate change, Rosa Luxemburg's assertion, that we face the choice of barbarism or socialism, rings true now more than ever.

If we accept that premise, to return to where I began, one cannot be a social justice activist without equally being an ecological justice activist; and link arms with all those fighting racist environmental violence the world over.

Ultimately, all of this can only be solved by the self-emancipation of humanity and putting in place a system that prioritizes long-term human and planetary health; real, bottom-up democracy based on cooperation; and production for human needs at its center. We need a system of cooperative and meaningful production, whereby the goal of society is social equity and ecological sustainability, and where environmental violence, in all its manifestations, is a thing of the past. To bring this about will require a social and ecological revolution. While we organize and fight for that future, we must simultaneously work to bring about the small victories, necessary to make people's immediate lives better and less polluted under capitalism, organize, and gain confidence for the larger, longer-term, and more profound and revolutionary battles to come.

9

AIG, Greed, and Legislative Stupidity

Jeb Golinkin

Jeb Golinkin is a contributing writer for The Week *and a former editor and reporter for the conservative blog* Frum Forum/New Majority.

The financial crisis was not the fault of greedy bank executives— they were simply acting as their shareholders expected, doing whatever they deemed necessary to maximize profits. Rather, it was, and continues to be, the government's lack of a regulatory regime that encourages positive, rather than harmful, corporate decision-making.

On Tuesday, Washington was abuzz with murmurs that AIG—the catastrophically managed insurer of untold amounts of Wall Street mortgage debt that required a $182 billion bailout in 2008—may join a $25 billion lawsuit against the United States government (i.e., the taxpayer) over the terms of that bailout. Outrage—manufactured and genuine— ensued.

The Tea Party crowd will undoubtedly go insane if the AIG board does in fact join Hank Greenberg and Co.'s lawsuit against the government. But a group of congressional Democrats—including Wall Street's least favorite senator, Elizabeth Warren, the always animated Maxine Waters, and three run-of-the-mill House Democrats—were the first leaders to publicly react to the news of the potential lawsuit. It seems that the Democratic lawmakers are surprised that a firm that was so recently saved by American taxpayers would even consider suing these same taxpayers. This confusion shows how little our leaders have learned about how corporations work.

Our leaders and citizens continue to believe the financial crisis was created by nothing more than immoral, greedy investment bankers. They are mistaken. Indeed, the financial crisis was not caused by a band of irrational, greedy fools, but rather by some of the smartest people in the United States acting exactly as we might have expected them to act had we taken a disinterested look at the incentives the legal and regulatory framework provided them. That we have not come to terms with this unpleasant reality is underscored by Congress' typically hasty reaction to the crisis. Contrary to the claims of the lawmakers responsible for passing Dodd-Frank, no less an expert than Weil's Harvey Miller, probably the top bankruptcy lawyer in the United States, maintains that the law has not so much as made a dent in the systemic risk posed by financial institutions that were and remain too big to fail.

It is . . . time for everyone to move past the incorrect and dramatically oversimplified idea that the financial crisis of 2008 was precipitated by a bunch of irrational, greedy, stupid bankers.

Of course, despite all of the huffing and puffing going on inside the Beltway, *DealBreaker*'s Matt Levine correctly points out that AIG will almost certainly not join the lawsuit. Aside from the fact that doing so would bring an immense amount of bad publicity to a company that is not exactly beloved by the public at large, the lawsuit appears to be a loser. The suit, the brainchild of former AIG CEO and "Master of the Universe" Hank Greenberg, failed before the United States District Court for the Southern District of New York. Greenberg's latest attempt, which is before the Court of Federal Claims in Washington, D.C., is unlikely to fare much better. The board, therefore, will probably elect not to join the lawsuit.

But what if the lawsuit did present a real chance of actual recovery for the shareholders? What then? Would it be acceptable for AIG's board to sue the very government that saved it from liquidation? The congressional Democrats who have chimed in so far certainly seem to think not. After ripping into the company and exclaiming that it should be taxed more in the future, Sen. Warren stated that "AIG should thank American taxpayers for their help, not bite the hand that fed them for helping them out in a crisis." Rep. Waters, the ranking Democratic member on the House Financial Services Committee, was even less circumspect, stating that she would "urge the board to drop its consideration of the lawsuit, thank the American public for the $182 billion rescue package that prevented the company's collapse, and support the reforms in the Dodd-Frank Wall Street Reform and Consumer Protection Act that ensure that systemically important financial institutions can no longer hold our economy hostage." Finally, and most notably, three congressional Democrats—Peter Welch, Michael Capuano, and Luis Gutierrez—sent AIG chair Robert S. Miller a letter in which they very thoughtfully state: "Don't do it. Don't even think about it."

So long as our lawmakers continue to rant and rail about "corporate greed" rather than addressing the incentives problem, we will never have a regulatory regime that encourages less risky decision-making.

Like any taxpayer, I am a bit irked with the possibility that after having bailed out AIG, the U.S. government might also have to defend a lawsuit against the company for not being generous enough. That said, and this is important, anyone who thinks that the government or the public ought to have any say in the board's decision is mistaken. Contrary to the sentiments expressed by leaders like Rep. Waters and Sen. Warren, the government has no more a right to make business decisions for private companies today than it did prior to the financial crisis. The basic rules have not changed. Financial institutions are just as free to act selfishly (at least from the non-shareholder's perspective) as they have ever been. In fact, if AIG's board were actually stupid enough to listen to Rep. Waters and blindly supported every crazy idea for "reforming" Wall Street she and her fellow members of Congress came up with, or refused to consider suing the government, as Reps. Welch, Capuano, and Gutierrez command in their letter, the board would be breaking the law by breaching their fiduciary duty to the shareholders who own their company.

We should not be surprised or disappointed that AIG is considering screwing the taxpayer to enrich itself. We want our corporations acting to maximize their own value using every lawful means at their disposal. That is what they exist to do. When corporations do well, they create jobs and stimulate economic growth, which is the only way we will ever emerge from the seemingly endless amounts of government debt we have piled up since the turn of the century. It is also time for everyone to move past the incorrect and dramatically over-simplified idea that the financial crisis of 2008 was precipitated by a bunch of irrational, greedy, stupid bankers who didn't care about whether they blew up the economy or not. If you want to explain the financial crisis to your 6-year-old in those terms, go for it. But that is not what happened. Indeed, given the systemic incentives in place prior to 2008, it is little wonder how any of us expected the outcome to be different. In his book on the financial crisis, *A Failure of Capitalism*, Judge Richard Posner (a conservative judicial icon and one of the few true public intellectuals of our time), wrote that bankers reacted much as we should have expected them to given the incentives built into the financial system. Bankers exist to maximize profits. Regulators exist to protect the social welfare from overly ambitious bankers. We do not need "more responsible" or "less greedy" bankers. We need regulations that understand reality—that dollars drive corporate decision-making—and use it to incentivize corporations to make decisions that promote financial stability and minimize systemic risk. In other words, we need a regulatory regime that seeks to align private profit motives with society's desire to promote stability.

We do not have such a regulatory regime, and so long as our lawmakers continue to rant and rail about "corporate greed" rather than addressing the incentives problem, we will never have a regulatory regime that encourages less risky decision-making. The problem is not greed. Indeed, if anything, greed can be part of the solution. Our nation's founders understood this, and created a system of law that channeled that avariciousness in ways that promoted the common good. It is time for our lawmakers to stop complaining that men are not angels and instead start doing what they should have done long ago, which is appoint a commission composed of the best minds on both sides of the aisle to go through every financial regulation, eliminate the ones that are not needed, and recommend the ones that are. In the meantime, they should stop yelling at AIG's board for fulfilling its legal obligations to its shareholders.

10

Government Policies, Not Greed, Caused the Financial Crisis

Norbert J. Michel

Norbert J. Michel is a research fellow in financial regulations for The Heritage Foundation and former professor of finance, economics, and statistics at Nicholls State University College of Business.

The financial crisis was created by a series of bad government policies that lowered mortgage standards and allowed too many unqualified buyers to purchase homes. The very same policies that helped to create the housing bubble are still in place and must be reformed in order to prevent another economic disaster.

In his State of the Union address last week [January 2015], President [Barack] Obama argued we need government polices to build "the most competitive economy anywhere." He's wrong. We need the government to leave the private sector alone so that it can build the most competitive economy anywhere.

The President and his supporters don't want to admit it, but the anemic recovery they're happily taking credit for comes on the heels of a financial crisis that was caused by a host of terrible government policies.

Federal Policies Caused Financial Crisis

Virtually every aspect of the meltdown can be traced to federal policies, many of which were designed to boost home mortgages. It's all laid out in *Hidden In Plain Sight: What Really Caused the Worlds' Worst Financial Crisis and Why it Could Happen Again*, a new book by [American Enterprise Institute] AEI's Peter Wallison. It's a must read for anyone who wants the straight dope on what caused the 2008 crisis.

Wallison's book is a valuable corrective, because too many policymakers have been getting away with a false narrative. These officials want us to believe the crisis had nothing to do with the government's affordable housing goals, and that deregulation and private-sector greed caused the meltdown.

Yet the financial crisis was, in truth, firmly rooted in a set of ill-conceived government policies that allowed too many people to take out home mortgages.

The practice of using federal agencies to make it easier for citizens to finance homes dates to the 1930s, and the 1977 Community Reinvestment Act significantly extended that idea. But then the S&Ls [Savings and Loans banks] crashed in the late 1980s, and federal meddling in the mortgage market really took off.

S&Ls had long served as a principal source of home financing in the U.S. Their demise created a huge void, one that the government sponsored enterprise (GSE) Fannie Mae was only too happy to fill.

Fannie [Mae] partnered with President Bill Clinton in what should be the textbook case for why it is so important to keep government officials out of the private sector.

And there's no doubt Fannie Mae's managers used the company's special government relationship to their advantage. For years, the company had used its ostensible affordable housing mission to fend off efforts to fully privatize its operations. Fannie's brass shored up their political cover in 1992 when they successfully lobbied Congress for explicit affordable housing goals.

In fact, *The New York Times* reported (in 1991) that the GSEs literally wrote much of the bill that required HUD [Housing and Urban Development] to establish three explicit affordable housing goals for the GSEs.

Soon after, Fannie partnered with President Bill Clinton in what should be the textbook case for why it is so important to keep government officials out of the private sector. Clinton's 1994 National Partners in Homeownership, a private-public cooperative, arbitrarily set a goal of raising the U.S. homeownership rate from 64 percent to 70 percent by 2000.

To complete its part of the deal, Fannie Mae announced its Trillion Dollar Commitment, a program that earmarked $1 trillion for affordable housing between 1994 and 2000.

Lower Credit Standards Increased Risky Home Loans

It shouldn't surprise anyone this policy ended badly. For starters, there was a good reason the home ownership rate had steadied near the 64 percent mark: the private mortgage marketplace had already helped most qualified borrowers buy a home.

The only way the GSEs could meet their affordable goals was to lower their credit standards, so that's exactly what they did. Wallison's book documents this fact by citing numerous government officials and GSE executives.

These lower standards became an even bigger problem because the GSEs' underwriting guidelines drove the entire home-financing market. That is, even standards for loans that weren't typically sold to Fannie and Freddie were influenced by the GSEs' guidelines.

I've witnessed several people deny this claim, but it's fully documented in Wallison's book.

The goals and the lower standards were bad enough on their own, but their impact was magnified because of other government policies. These policies ensured that risky mortgages would be spread throughout the financial system and magnify any liquidity problems that mortgage defaults may cause.

The short version deals with the Basel capital requirements, a set of rules that the federal government imposed on U.S. commercial banks in the late 1980s.

These rules sought to better match capital to the risk level of banks' assets. That is, they tried to reduce the amount of capital banks held based on the perceived riskiness of specific bank assets.

[Government] policies served to standardize the market and fill it with mortgages that, only a few years prior, would have been deemed high risk.

From the beginning, the rules provided capital relief to banks that held GSE-issued mortgage-backed securities (MBS). Then, in 2001, the Federal Reserve (jointly with the FDIC [Federal Deposit Insurance Corporation] and OCC [Office of the Comptroller of the Currency]) amended the rules to provide even more capital relief.

The 2001 rule change, known as the recourse rule, gave certain highly-rated, privately issued MBS the same low-risk weight as the GSE-issued MBS.

These rules provided private firms with an added incentive to securitize mortgages, and also gave banks a strong incentive to securitize, rather than hold, their mortgages. The capital rules took effect just as the affordable housing goals provided the GSEs a strong incentive to finance even more mortgages.

Combined, these policies served to standardize the market and fill it with mortgages that, only a few years prior, would have been deemed high risk.

Arbitrary Home Ownership Goals Created the Housing Bubble

Some may find it ironic that these policies, in the name of making housing more affordable, created a housing bubble. But there's nothing unexpected about the sharp increase in housing prices these policies produced.

Start with a completely arbitrary goal of increasing home ownership when most qualified homebuyers already own homes. Add to the mix government-sanctioned, if not imposed, lower credit standards along with abundant financing.

For good measure, throw in government-imposed capital requirements that all but beg companies to hold the MBS tied to these lower quality mortgages.

One doesn't need a Ph.D. in economics to predict this combination of policies will lead to higher consumer debt, higher home prices, and an unstable financial system.

The scary thing is that the system that gave us the crisis— affordable housing goals, shaky underwriting standards, and the GSEs—remains largely in place.

These policies need to be reversed if we want to prevent another crisis. A roadmap for doing just that is contained in The Heritage Foundation's new guide to federal policy reform: "Opportunity for All, Favoritism to None."

11

Corporate Rights Endanger People's Constitutional Rights

Ron Fein

Ron Fein is an attorney and legal director for Free Speech for People, a legal advocacy organization based in Austin, Texas.

Corporations, who already receive many special advantages and privileges, are becoming increasingly litigious with regard to their perceived constitutional rights, especially concerning freedom of speech and freedom of religion—rights that had previously been reserved for individuals. The judicial system must delineate between the freedoms the US Constitution grants to people versus those it grants to corporations.

Four years after the Supreme Court's [2010] ruling in *Citizens United [v. Federal Election Commission]*, most Americans are revolted at the scale of campaign spending ushered in by the decision and dismayed by a political system they view as favoring the wealthy. They remain suspicious that somehow these flaws in our democracy have made solutions to the problems of unemployment, income inequality, global warming and a host of others elusive, and perhaps impossible, for our leaders to find.

Most Americans, however, have yet to realize just how destructive the ideas driving *Citizens United* really are—and how several cases the Supreme Court is set to decide this year [2014] could have the power to exacerbate the problems we face and create dangerous precedents that will harm our democracy and our society for years to come.

The Rise of the Corporate Rights Doctrine

Conestoga Wood Specialties v. Sebelius is one of those cases. Arising from a challenge to the Affordable Care Act by the kitchen cabinet manufacturer, it asks whether a corporation can be compelled to provide its employees with health care that includes coverage for contraception if the corporate shareholders have a religious objection. On March 25 [2014], the Supreme Court is scheduled to hear arguments in this case, along with a similar case, *Sebelius v. Hobby Lobby*.

The troubling new trend that most Americans have yet to recognize is the extension of constitutional rights, such as freedom of speech or religion, to corporations.

But these cases are about more than Obamacare, just as *Citizens United* is about more than money in politics. The same extraordinary claim made in *Citizens United*—that corporations are entitled to the same constitutional rights as people—is at the heart of *Conestoga*. Four years ago, corporations cemented a claim to the right of free speech under the First Amendment, and now corporations are hoping to capture religious freedom as well.

The very fact that a cabinet door manufacturer has made it to the Supreme Court by claiming religious freedom shows how far the flawed doctrine of "corporate rights" has come. Yet the doctrine is hardly new. Increasingly, corporations have claimed First Amendment rights as a means to strike down laws that their managers view as unfavorable to the bottom line. Over time, they have racked up a dangerous record of success, using the courts to invalidate laws enacted by our democratically elected representatives to protect the public interest.

The corporate rights doctrine is based on a truly radical idea of what corporations actually are. Corporations are economic entities, chartered by the state for the purpose of making money. They serve a necessary and useful role in our society, a role we facilitate by granting them many privileges, such as perpetual life, limited liability, and often, special tax advantages. Corporations have always had legal rights, and they exercise those rights all the time to operate effectively in the economy.

"We the Corporations"

The troubling new trend that most Americans have yet to recognize is the extension of constitutional rights, such as freedom of speech or religion, to corporations. The Bill of Rights is so vital because it protects these freedoms for "We the People." Transferring those constitutional rights to "We the Corporations" is done at the expense of the people and the public interest.

Millions will be spent in the 2014 election cycle, most likely more than has ever been spent on politics in the history of any country. Much of this, of course, is thanks to *Citizens United*, which, just four years after it emerged, has flooded our politics with campaign money, undermined our democracy, and made the real problems we face harder to solve.

But the other harsh legacy may be the way *Citizens United* has set the legal table for future decisions like *Conestoga*. The Supreme Court must be aware of just how profoundly its coming decisions will shape our country. Granting more and more constitutional rights to the economic actors known as corporations would, in the end, leave us with fewer for ourselves.

12

Corporate Rights Do Not Endanger People's Constitutional Rights

Kenneth Bennight

Kenneth Bennight is a Texas-based attorney and contributor to the conservative publication American Thinker.

Corporations are created and governed by people, and as such they should be afforded the opportunity to speak collectively in defense of their interests. These corporations, however, are often unfairly maligned for expecting the US Constitution to uphold their rights.

Ron Fein is the legal director for Free Speech for People. He recently [January 16, 2014] wrote an opinion column decrying the argument that corporations have First Amendment rights. But the column is simplistic and conclusory. Few argue that corporations should have all the constitutional rights of individuals just as few argue they should have no rights at all.

If you prefer a system in which corporations have no rights, then you shut down the economy. With no rights, corporations could not enforce contracts, and governments could take their property without compensation. I doubt Mr. Fein believes that is a good idea, and even if he does, he neglects to say so. Doing otherwise would be poor salesmanship.

If we are to accord corporations some rights and not others, we ought to have a basis other than using the term "corporation" as an epithet and moving on. Deciding what First-Amendment protections corporations should have is complex. In addressing that complexity, the first step is to separate two rights Mr. Fein lumps together: freedom of speech and freedom of religion.

Corporations and Freedom of Speech

Corporate freedom of speech is different from corporate freedom of religion. Government has long intertwined itself into the workings of the economy. The intertwining accelerated at times, such as under Woodrow Wilson and Franklin Roosevelt, and slowed at others. It always continued, however, and we are in a new period of acceleration under the current administration. All participants in the economy naturally want some say in how the government affects them.

Prohibiting corporations from participating in public debate is akin to imposing an arms embargo on rebels resisting a tyrant.

In assessing corporate participation in public debate, consider what corporations are. Corporations are formed by people to advance their economic interests. Limited liability is an advantage even when the corporation has only one shareholder, but limited liability also makes it possible for many people to pool their money to support an enterprise. When people pool their money to act collectively, why should they not be able to speak collectively when government threatens their collective interests?

Take hydraulic fracturing as an example. Many want to regulate it more heavily, and maybe doing so is appropriate. But heavy regulation uninformed by how the business works might shut down or unnecessarily impair an activity with important benefits to society as a whole. Oil companies are the mechanism by which those who have invested in the oil business pursue their economic interests. Silencing oil companies in the hydraulic-fracturing debate would hobble one side.

The same principle applies throughout the economy. Individual shareholders often lack the means and, depending on the size of their investment, the incentive to participate in a public debate. Those who do participate are decried as the evil rich. The [Republican billionaire] Koch brothers [Charles and David] are an example, though the same standard seems not to apply to [liberal billionaire] George Soros. Prohibiting corporations from participating in public debate is akin to imposing an arms embargo on rebels resisting a tyrant. It makes a given outcome significantly more likely. Society as a whole, as opposed to partisans within it, has no basis to silence one side of a debate.

Corporations and Freedom of Religion

Freedom of religion is a separate topic. It is hard to see a genuine religious concern of a publicly traded company. Those are the corporations many want you to think of when they decry corporate religious freedom. But most corporations are small and closely held. Some argue that, merely because Tom the electrician operates on a corporate basis, he must forfeit all religious concerns in conducting his business. Really? Why should that be so? That is at least a topic for genuine debate.

Mr. Fein specifically mentions Hobby Lobby and Conestoga Wood Specialties. These are larger than the electrician example, but I generally understand them to be family-held companies. I do not want to defend the merits of their specific claims, about which I know little. Unlike Mr. Fein, however, I believe courts should assess the claims instead of rejecting them merely because a corporation is involved. How that assessment should come out. I do not know.

It's hard not to believe that many who agree with Mr. Fein would take a contrary position if the issue arose in the context of corporations opposing military action. Then we might hear how brave and transgressive it is to assert religious principles. The same principles ought to apply in that case as in the Affordable Care Act.

The U.S. Court of Appeals for the Fourth Circuit recently upheld a corporate assertion of what one might consider a personal right. Carnell Construction Corporation, an African-American-owned enterprise, accused the Danville Redevelopment and Housing Authority of racial discrimination in administering a contract. I do not know whether Carnell was discriminated against, but I see no problem with it being able to litigate whether it was. And if, as the Fourth Circuit stated, Carnell can have an imputed racial identity, why should all corporations necessarily be barred from asserting an imputed religious identity?

Too often in public discussion, the word "corporation" is used as an epithet. That is destructive to reasoned discourse. Corporations are no more or less evil than the people behind them. We would all be better off if public debate focused on substance and not name-calling.

Organizations to Contact

The editors have compiled the following list of organizations concerned with the issues debated in this book. The descriptions are derived from materials provided by the organizations. All have publications or information available for interested readers. The list was compiled on the date of publication of the present volume; the information provided here may change. Be aware that many organizations take several weeks or longer to respond to inquiries, so allow as much time as possible.

AFL-CIO
815 16th St. NW, Washington, DC   20006
(202) 637-5000
website: www.aflcio.org

The AFL-CIO is a federation of fifty-six labor unions representing 12.5 million workers in the United States that seeks to bring economic and social justice to workplaces and communities across the country. The organization lobbies the White House, the US Congress, and state legislatures on behalf of working Americans to ensure that all people who work receive decent paychecks and benefits, safe jobs, respect, and fair treatment. The AFL-CIO website includes a section entitled Corporate Watch, which offers links to its Executive Paywatch and Capital Stewardship programs, as well as links to resources that unions and community activists can use to research their own companies. Executive Paywatch monitors the salaries and retirement packages of chief executive officers in relation to the American workforce.

America's Watchdog
5614 Connecticut Ave. NW, Suite 138, Washington, DC   20015
(866) 714-6466 • fax: (206) 299-4440
e-mail: AmericasWatchdog@aol.com
website: http://americaswatchdog.com

America's Watchdog is a national advocacy organization for consumer protection and corporate fair play. The group serves as the parent organization for a number of consumer advocacy initiatives, including ones dealing with corporate accountability, such as the Banks Watchdog, Corporate Whistle Blower Center, False Labelling Complaint Center, and the Wall Street Fraud Watchdog. Each of these programs has its own web page within the parent website of America's Watchdog and typically includes links to actions and investigations the program has successfully conducted, as well as press releases for the media and general public.

Business Roundtable
300 New Jersey Ave. NW, Suite 800, Washington, DC   20001
(202) 872-1260
e-mail: info@brt.org
website: http://businessroundtable.org

The Business Roundtable is an association of chief executive officers of leading US companies that seeks to promote sound public policy and a thriving US economy. It conducts research, publishes position papers, and advocates public policies that support economic growth, a dynamic global economy, and a productive US workforce. The Business Roundtable's website includes links to a variety of reports and research papers the group has produced in the areas of corporate governance and corporate regulation.

Center for Corporate Policy
PO Box 19405, Washington, DC   20036
(202) 387-8030 • fax: (202) 234-5176
e-mail: ruskin@corporatepolicy.org
website: www.corporatepolicy.org

The Center for Corporate Policy is a nonprofit, nonpartisan public interest organization working to curb corporate abuses and make corporations publicly accountable. The Center works to achieve public and government action in the areas of corporate crime and abuse, excessive executive compensation, corporate monopolization and antitrust, and the unconstitutional expansion of corporate rights in courts and legislatures. The Center's website includes links to news and articles focusing on corporate crime and abuse, as well as links to external blogs, reports, organizations, and other resources dealing with corporate corruption.

Center for Public Integrity

910 17th St. NW, Suite 700, Washington, DC   20006
(202) 466-1300
website: www.publicintegrity.org

The Center for Public Integrity is one of the oldest and largest nonpartisan, nonprofit investigative news organizations in the United States. Its mission is to serve democracy by revealing abuses of power, corruption, and betrayal of public trust by powerful public and private institutions, using the tools of investigative journalism. The Center focuses its investigations on the following areas: money and politics; government waste, fraud, and abuse; the environment; health-care reform; national security; and state government transparency. One of the Center's key projects is the International Consortium of Investigative Journalists, which consists of 160 reporters in sixty countries who collaborate on in-depth investigative stories and further the Center's mission as a watchdog organization.

Citizen Works

PO Box 18478, Washington, DC   20036
(202) 265-6164
e-mail: information@citizenworks.org
website: http://citizenworks.org

Citizen Works is a nonprofit, nonpartisan organization founded by Ralph Nader in 2001 to advance justice by strengthening citizen participation in power. It seeks to give people the tools and opportunities to build democracy and to develop innovative and systemic means to advance the progressive citizen movement. Citizen Works operates a number of programs that address various aspects of corporate corruption, including the Association for Integrity of Accounting, the Campaign for Corporate Reform, and a campaign to end corporate executive greed. The group also publishes such handbooks, reports, and fact sheets as *The People's Business, Citizens Working* newsletter, *Challenging Corporate Power Handbook*, corporate power scandal sheets, corporate power fact sheets, and corporate tax traitors, some of which are available at its website.

The Conference Board

835 Third Ave., New York, NY   10022-6600
(212) 759-0900
website: www.conference-board.org

Founded in 1916, the Conference Board is a global, independent business membership and research association working in the public interest. Its mission is to provide the world's leading organizations with the practical knowledge they need to improve their performance and better serve society. The Conference Board works within and across three main subject areas—Corporate Leadership, Economy & Business Environment, and Human Capital—to create a unique, enterprise-wide perspective that helps business leaders make the right strategic decisions every day. The organization produces a number of publications and reports that focus on issues of corporate accountability as well as webcasts that deal specifically with corporate governance.

Consumer Watchdog

2701 Ocean Park Blvd., Suite 112, Santa Monica, CA   90405
(310) 392-0522
e-mail: admin@consumerwatchdog.org
website: www.consumerwatchdog.org

Consumer Watchdog is a nonprofit organization dedicated to providing an effective voice for taxpayers and consumers in an era when special interests dominate public discourse, government, and politics. The organization deploys an in-house team of public interest lawyers, policy experts, strategists, and grassroots activists to expose, confront, and change corporate and political injustice in the United States, saving Americans billions of dollars and improving countless lives. Consumer Watchdog addresses a number of issues important to consumers, including protecting health-care patients, insurance reform, and fighting the corporate assault against individual rights and freedoms. The group's website includes numerous blogs, press releases, podcasts, and videos dealing with different instances of corporate corruption.

Corporate Accountability International

10 Milk St., Suite 610, Boston, MA   02108
(617) 695-2525
e-mail: info@stopcorporateabuse.org
website: www.stopcorporateabuse.org

Corporate Accountability International works to safeguard public health, human rights, and the environment from corporate abuse. It is committed to stopping life-threatening abuses by global corporations and increasing their accountability to public institutions and people around the world. The organization currently operates four main campaigns: challenge corporate control of the world's water; challenge corporate abuse of our food supplies; challenge the multinational tobacco industry; and administer the "Corporate Hall of Shame," which works with allied organizations and voters to confront corporations that corrupt the political process, abuse human rights, and devastate the environment. Corporate Accountability's website includes a number of useful resources on corporate abuse, including its quarterly newsletter, *Spotlight*, and various reports and publications, all of which are available to download for free.

Corporate Watch

c/o Freedom Press, Angel Alley, 84b Whitechapel High St.
London   E1 7QX
   United Kingdom
+44(0) 207 426 0005

e-mail: contact@corporatewatch.org
website: www.corporatewatch.org

Corporate Watch is an independent research group that investigates the social and environmental impacts of corporations and corporate power. Corporate Watch strives for a society that is truly democratic, equitable, nonexploitative, and ecologically sustainable. The group maintains that progress toward such a society can only be achieved through dismantling the vast economic and political power that corporations have come to exert, as well as developing alternatives to the present socio-economic system. Corporate Watch has a variety of books, reports, and videos, including its magazine *Corporate Watch*, available on its website.

CorpWatch

PO Box 29198, San Francisco, CA   94129
(415) 226-6226
website: http://corpwatch.org

CorpWatch is a nonprofit investigative research organization that works to expose corporate malfeasance and to advocate for multinational corporate accountability and transparency. The group acts to foster global justice, independent media activism, and democratic control over corporations. It also seeks to expose multinational corporations that profit from war, fraud, environmental, human rights, and other abuses, and to provide critical information to foster a more informed public and an effective democracy. CorpWatch focuses its activities on the following key issues: consumerism and commercialism; corporate corruption; environmental exploitation; excessive executive compensation; globalization; health care; human rights; labor rights; money and politics; privatization of the public sector; regulation; trade justice; and world financial institutions. The CorpWatch website includes an interactive research guide that helps activists research a corporation's business strategy, financial status, and environmental and social record. The site also includes links to numerous articles on current issues of corporate abuse and a blog written by CorpWatch staff.

Council of Better Business Bureaus (CBBB)
3033 Wilson Blvd., Suite 600, Arlington, VA 22201
(703) 276-0100
website: www.bbb.org/council

The Council of Better Business Bureaus (CBBB) is the national "network hub" for the 112 Better Business Bureaus located across the United States. A nonprofit organization, CBBB is one of the nation's recognized leaders in developing and administering self-regulation programs for the business community. The core mission of the Better Business Bureau is to advance trust in the commerce marketplace, which it does by setting standards for marketplace trust; encouraging and supporting best practices by engaging with and educating consumers and businesses; celebrating marketplace role models; calling out and addressing substandard marketplace behavior; and creating a community of trustworthy businesses and charities. The CBBB website offers information for both consumers and businesses, including tips to avoid scams and an online form for filing a complaint against a business.

CSRwire
c/o 3BL Media, 16 Center St., Suite 211
Northampton, MA 01060
(802) 251-0110
e-mail: info@csrwire.com
website: www.csrwire.com

Founded in 1999, CSRwire is a digital media platform for the latest news, views, and reports in corporate social responsibility (CSR) and sustainability. CSRwire has helped to pave the way for new standards of corporate citizenship, earning the international respect of thought leaders, business leaders, academics, researchers, activists, and the media. The CSRwire team works on a wide range of traditional and social media services and solutions to support its members' marketing and communications strategies. The organization's website includes information on CSR events, news, reports, books, and a blog written by CSR thought leaders and the reading public.

Ethics and Compliance Initiative (ECI)
2345 Crystal Dr., Suite 201, Arlington, VA   22202
(703) 647-2185 • fax: (703) 647-2180
e-mail: ethics@ethics.org
website: www.ethics.org

The Ethics and Compliance Initiative (ECI) is a nonprofit organization that advances research, knowledge, and implementation of practices that promote excellence in ethics and compliance programs. ECI was formed by the alliance of the Ethics Resource Center and the Ethics and Compliance Officer Association. ECI, through three organizational areas, conducts research, publishes white papers, encourages best practices, and offers educational resources and online forums to help the ethics and compliance industry. The group's website includes a link to resources such as ethics publications, articles, surveys, and an ethics toolkit.

International Forum on Globalization (IFG)
1009 General Kennedy Ave., San Francisco, CA   94129
(415) 561-7650
e-mail: ifg@ifg.org
website: http://ifg.org

The International Forum on Globalization (IFG) is a research and educational institution composed of leading activists, economists, scholars, and researchers providing analysis and critiques on the cultural, social, political, and environmental impacts of economic globalization. The IFG website includes numerous reports and publications that examine the impact of globalization on various social and environmental issues, including *Outing the Oligarchy: Billionaires Who Benefit from Today's Climate Crisis* and *Intrinsic Consequences of Economic Globalization on the Environment.*

US Securities and Exchange Commission (SEC)
100 F St. NE, Washington, DC   20549
(202) 942-8088
website: www.sec.gov

The US Securities and Exchange Commission (SEC) is the US government agency that oversees securities markets to protect investors and facilitate capital formation. The SEC oversees the key participants in the securities world, including securities exchanges, securities brokers and dealers, investment advisors, and mutual funds. Here the SEC is concerned primarily with promoting the disclosure of important market-related information, maintaining fair dealing, and protecting against fraud. Each year the SEC brings hundreds of civil enforcement actions against individuals and companies for violation of the securities laws. Under the Enforcement division of the SEC website there are numerous links to information about corporate and individual fraud cases being investigated or resolved by the agency.

Weinberg Center for Corporate Governance
Alfred Lerner College of Business and Economics
University of Delaware, Alfred Lerner Hall, Room 103
Newark, DE   19716
(302) 831-6157 • fax: (302) 831-6886
website: www.lerner.udel.edu/centers/weinberg

The Weinberg Center for Corporate Governance, within the University of Delaware's Alfred Lerner College of Business and Economics, seeks to enact progressive changes in corporate structure and management through education and interaction. The Center provides a forum for business leaders, corporate board members, the legal community, academics, practitioners, students, and others interested in corporate governance issues to meet, interact, learn, and teach. The Center's website includes links to numerous publications and reports dealing with issues of corporate governance, including such topics as executive compensation and board oversight.

Bibliography

Books

Liaquat Ahamed   *Lords of Finance: The Bankers Who Broke the World*. New York: Penguin Press, 2009.

Stephen V. Arbogast   *Resisting Corporate Corruption: Cases in Practical Ethics from Enron Through the Financial Crisis*. Hoboken, NJ: John Wiley & Sons, 2013.

Tom Burgis   *The Looting Machine: Warlords, Oligarchs, Corporations, Smugglers, and the Theft of Africa's Wealth*. New York: PublicAffairs, 2015.

Corporate Reform Collective   *Fighting Corporate Abuse: Beyond Predatory Capitalism*. London: Pluto Press, 2014.

Greg Farrell   *Corporate Crooks: How Rogue Executives Ripped Off Americans . . . and Congress Helped Them Do It!* New York: Prometheus Books, 2006.

Charles H. Ferguson   *Predator Nation: Corporate Criminals, Political Corruption, and the Hijacking of America*. New York: Crown Business, 2012.

Abraham L. Gitlow   *Corruption in Corporate America: Who Is Responsible? Who Will Protect the Public Interest?* Lanham, MD: University Press of America, 2005.

Arianna Huffington — *Pigs at the Trough: How Corporate Greed and Political Corruption Are Undermining America.* New York: Crown Publishers, 2003.

Laurence Leamer — *The Price of Justice: A True Story of Greed and Corruption.* New York: Times Books, 2013.

Edward C. Lorenz — *Civic Empowerment in the Age of Corporate Greed.* Lansing, MI: Michigan State University Press, 2012.

Jeff Madrick — *Age of Greed: The Triumph of Finance and the Decline of America, 1970 to the Present.* New York: Vintage Books, 2012.

Raymond J. Michalowski and Ronald C. Kramer, eds. — *State-Corporate Crime: Wrongdoing at the Intersection of Business and Government.* New Brunswick, NJ: Rutgers University Press, 2006.

Gretchen Morgenson and Joshua Rosner — *Reckless Endangerment: How Outsized Ambition, Greed, and Corruption Created the Worst Financial Crisis of Our Time.* New York: Times Books, 2011.

Robert B. Reich — *Beyond Outrage: What Has Gone Wrong with Our Economy and Our Democracy, and How to Fix It.* New York: Vintage Books, 2012.

Marie-Monique Robin — *The World According to Monsanto.* New York: The New Press, 2010.

Bernie Sanders   *The Speech: A Historic Filibuster on Corporate Greed and the Decline of Our Middle Class.* New York: Nation Books, 2011.

Greg Smith   *Why I Left Goldman Sachs: A Wall Street Story.* New York: Grand Central Publishing, 2012.

Jonathan Tasini   *The Audacity of Greed: Free Markets, Corporate Thieves, and the Looting of America.* Brooklyn, NY: Ig Publishing, 2009.

Zephyr Teachout   *Corruption in America: From Benjamin Franklin's Snuff Box to Citizens United.* Cambridge, MA: Harvard University Press, 2014.

Peter J. Wallison   *Hidden in Plain Sight: What Really Caused the World's Worst Financial Crisis and Why It Could Happen Again.* New York: Encounter Books, 2015.

Periodicals and Internet Sources

Ted Baumann   "'I Scratch Your Back, You Scratch Mine.' How Corporations Control the Government," *The Sovereign Investor Daily*, February 26, 2105. http://thesovereigninvestor.com.

Michael Blanding   "Is Corporate Corruption a Necessary Evil?," *Forbes*, November 24, 2014.

Chad Brooks   "Corporate Corruption Is a Global
                   Epidemic," *Business News Daily*, May
                   10, 2012. www.businessnewsdaily
                   .com.

Paul Buchheit   "5 Ways Our Lives Are Being
                   Violated by Corporate Greed,"
                   AlterNet, December 1, 2013.
                   www.alternet.org.

Sharan Burrow   "This May Day—End Corporate
                   Greed," *Huffington Post*, May 1, 2015.
                   www.huffingtonpost.com.

David Dayen   "Bank of America Whistleblower's
                   Bombshell: 'We Were Told to Lie,'"
                   Salon, June 18, 2103. www.salon.com.

Chris Dodd   "Why Dodd-Frank Is Necessary,"
                   Politico, July 22, 2012.
                   www.politico.com.

Jeffrey Dorfman   "Workers Should Be Very Thankful
                   That Corporations Are So Greedy,"
                   Forbes, December 15, 2013.

Economist   "The New Age of Crony Capitalism,"
                   March 15, 2014.

Nick Fillmore   "Price Paid for Corporate
                   Environmental Destruction,"
                   Dissident Voice, December 12, 2014.
                   http://dissidentvoice.org.

Leah McGrath   "Nonsensical Sentences for White
Goodman   Collar Criminals," *Newsweek*, June 26,
                   2014.

William Greider   "Why Don't White-Collar Criminals Get Equal Time?," *The Nation*, February 5, 2013.

Peter J. Henning   "Greed Continues to Fuel Penny Stock Frauds," *New York Times*, September 15, 2014.

Neil Irwin   "Americans Are O.K. with Big Business. It's Business Lobbying Power They Hate," *New York Times*, September 23, 2014.

Georg Kell   "Five Trends That Show Corporate Responsibility Is Here to Stay," *Guardian*, August 13, 2104.

Knowledge @Wharton   "Why the US Corporate World Became 'A Bull Market for Corruption,'" June 30, 2014. http://knowledge.wharton.upenn.edu.

Elizabeth Loftus   "The Giving Trees: Fighting Corruption in the Timber Industry with Technology," *GAB: The Global Anticorruption Blog*, January 5, 2105. http://globalanticorruptionblog.com.

Michel Martin   "Street Crime vs. Corporate Crime: Equally Judged?," NPR, July 18, 2011. www.npr.org.

Marcus Mayo   "Crony Capitalism or Just Plain Capitalism?," *Socialist Appeal*, May 16, 2014. http://socialistappeal.org.

Leonard McCarthy	"Has Globalization Made Corruption Worse?," World Economic Forum, October 24, 2014. https://agenda.weforum.org.
Bill Moyers and Michael Winship	"Corporate Greed Is Poisoning America—Literally," *Salon*, May 20, 2013. www.salon.com.
Ralph Nader	"Credit Suisse: Big Crimes Become Big Business," *Huffington Post*, January 16, 2105. www.huffingtonpost.com.
Joe Nocera	"C.E.O Pay Goes Up, Up and Away!," *New York Times*, April 14, 2014.
Brad Plumer	"The Economics of Corporate Crime," *Washington Post*, July 23, 2012.
Eduardo Porter	"The Spreading Scourge of Corporate Corruption," *New York Times*, July 10, 2012.
James R. Rogers	"The Benefits, and Costs, of Globalization," *First Things*, April 16, 2013. www.firstthings.com.
Jack Rothman	"Minimum Wage? How About a Maximum Wage?," *Huffington Post*, May 27, 2015. www.huffingtonpost .com.
Samuel Rubenfeld	"Corruption 'Isn't Just the Cost of Doing Business,'" *Wall Street Journal*, April 10, 2015. http://blogs.wsj.com.

Peter Schweizer   "'The Economist' Misses the Point on Crony Capitalism," Breitbart, March 17, 2014. www.breitbart.com.

Aaron Taube   "Maybe Occupy Wall Street Wasn't Such a Failure After All," *Business Insider*, September 17, 2103. www.businessinsider.com.

Ravi Venkatesan   "Confronting Corruption," *McKinsey Quarterly*, January 2015. www.mckinsey.com/insights.

Verité   "Corruption and Labor Trafficking in Global Supply Chains," December 2013. www.verite.org.

Heesun Wee   "Wall Street Greed, 5 Years After the Crash," Yahoo! Finance, September 13, 2013. http://finance.yahoo.com.

Christopher Whalen   "Washington & Wall Street: Dodd-Frank Will Cause the Next Financial Meltdown," Breitbart, September 16, 2013. www.breitbart.com.

Index

31901062613866

CPSIA information can be obtained
at www.ICGtesting.com
Printed in the USA
BVHW04s2256200318
511126BV00007B/229/P

9 780737 773651